The Long, Dark Tunnel

A Mother's Journey to Hell and Back

Thelma Wehunt

iUniverse, Inc.
Bloomington

The Long, Dark Tunnel
A Mother's Journey to Hell and Back

iUniverse books may be ordered through booksellers or by contacting:

iUniverse
1663 Liberty Drive
Bloomington, IN 47403
www.iuniverse.com
1-800-Authors (1-800-288-4677)

ISBN: 978-1-4759-2774-0 (sc)
ISBN: 978-1-4759-2776-4 (hc)
ISBN: 978-1-4759-2775-7 (e)

Printed in the United States of America

iUniverse rev. date: 5/18/2012

For my two beautiful daughters and my beautiful granddaughters, Ragina, Renee, and Jessica. I love you all very much.

Contents

Preface

If only I could tell every mother who has lost a child, "If you know God, it will be okay." Of course, it will never be okay, and you will never get over it. God will help you through it, but that does not happen overnight. It is a process. But if you know God, at least you can allow him to take you through it.

How do I know? Because I lost not only one child but both of my children, along with one of my grandchildren—and not over time but all at once, in a single, defining moment that sent me spiraling out of control, down an unmarked, unanticipated path and into a long, dark tunnel. Inside this tunnel, I found not only the unbearable grief of losing my daughters, who were also my best friends, but also the introduction of further turmoil, including by necessity taking custody of some of my grandchildren, physical trauma, the death of my mother, a harrowing court battle over my granddaughter, and the near-death of my husband. All of this resulted in an unsettled family life, even more heartache, piles of unpaid medical bills, and the loss of much of our personal property.

At the time, I was convinced that my only way out of this nightmarish tunnel would be the grave. But God, in his infinite wisdom, had other ideas. In some imperceptible way, over the course of nearly eight years, he led me through the impossible conditions of that dark place and out into the rest of my life.

I still struggle, sometimes daily, and what lies in the future, I do not know. But I do know a few things: (1) God will show me where to go from here, albeit one day at a time, which is the only way I can face living anyway, and (2) he was with me all along. There were times when

I was sure I was all alone and that God had forgotten about my pain. But he hadn't. That's why I am now sharing my experiences with you.

If you are, or know, a parent who is dealing with the aftermath of the loss of a child or other loved one, I am here to tell you that if God was able to bring me through my torturous circumstances, he can bring you through too. I am here to remind you that when there seems to be only one set of footprints in the sand, it is because he is carrying you. So many times while in the tunnel, I forgot that. But now, as I look back, I can see that I was never really alone, because if I had been, I would not have made it out.

My prayer is that, by reading this book, you will be able to regain hope, along with the realization that God will never put more upon you than he will give you strength to bear. I also pray that it might help you realize, or maybe just remember, that the choice to live again is in your hands. You alone must choose God, and you alone must find the courage to decide to allow your circumstances to make you better and not bitter.

If I can give even one person hope in a time of pain, then my efforts will not have been in vain. Giving such a gift is one way I can honor the memory of my beautiful daughters and granddaughter, who are now together enjoying the beauty of heaven.

Acknowledgments

Being in the family I am in is the greatest blessing of all. My sisters, nieces, and nephews are such a miracle. I would not be here writing this today if they were not in my life.

Also I want to thank the travelers from all over the United States who helped with their giving and most of all their love and prayers. I want to thank all the wonderful people in Spiro who came to us in Amarillo. I'd also like to thank Robert and Madge Cooper, who came from Colorado and set up the bank account. There is no way I could mention all the names of the wonderful people in Spiro, Oklahoma, who blessed us. I'd just like to say I was so blessed to be your pastor, and you will always be in my heart and part of my family.

Part I

From Light into Darkness

Once Upon a Time

Train up a child in the way he should go:
and when he is old, he will not depart from it.
—Proverbs 22:6

My first daughter died at birth. I named her Debbie. It has been forty-eight years, and I still think of her. Four years later, on October 14, 1965, God gave me Ragina, and what a blessing she was to my life. She did not take the place of Debbie but came with her own gift of love. That was the happiest day I can remember. That is, until December 17, 1968, when Renee came on the scene. My goodness, she looked just like Ragina! Renee also came with her own gift of love, as one child never takes the place of another. Instead, each has a special place in a mother's heart. From that day forward, it was the three of us.

Ragina was three when Renee was born, and she always wanted to be wherever Renee was—and I mean that literally. It wasn't enough for Renee to be in the same room as Ragina or even in the same general area. Renee had to be right next to her sister all the time. If Ragina was on the south end of the couch, that is the end Ragina wanted to be on. Even when Renee was in her baby bed, that is where Ragina wanted to be. It was impossible to keep the two of them apart, so I never tried. Even when they became older, they always stuck together. As teenagers, they double-dated. Whatever one could not think of, the other one did. As adults, whether it was shopping, going to church, or just being at each others' houses watching kids, they were inseparable. Most of my pictures of the girls are of them together.

All through their childhood, keeping them in church was my main goal. As long as it was in my power, I made them go to church. I also made sure to tell them about God and to teach them that Jesus was the only way to salvation. God knows I made my share of mistakes, and more, but when all was said and done, they still knew the love of God—and they knew that no matter how hard life got, God was the answer.

As they got older, there were some bad moments. At times it was only the three of us, but we never lost each other. We were always there for the others, no matter what. I lived in an abusive relationship for many years, and I had to get me and my girls out of the situation. As a mother, I always did what I thought was best at the time, and somehow our bond, along with my efforts, helped us muddle through.

Then in 1986, I received the strangest phone call, not knowing at the time it was going to change my life. It was a beautiful night. I had just returned home from church when my phone rang. I rushed to answer, as I was just coming in the door. I said hello, and a voice I did not know said,

"Hello, is your name Thelma McAdoo?"

I replied, "Yes."

The voice asked, "Was your dad a preacher?"

"Yes."

"Did he die?"

"Yes." By this time I was thinking, *This person sure knows a lot about me. I hope he's not a stalker or worse.* I asked, "Who is this?"

He replied with another question: "Do you know Theadore Wehunt?"

Now, with excitement in my voice, I said, "Yes, all my life."

"Well, do you know his son Kenny?"

Now I was not feeling so much excitement, because I didn't like Ken when we were kids and was sure it would not be any different now. I said, "Yes."

He then said, "It is me."

I was shocked and wondering, *What in the name of God is he doing calling me? I haven't even seen him in about fifteen years.* All of this was going through my mind.

Then he said, "I was wondering if I flew to Oklahoma to take you out to dinner if you would go."

I thought for a second and then said, "If you are stupid enough to fly to Oklahoma to take me out to eat, I would probably be stupid enough to go."

He did, I did, and that is how we all became a family. However, my girls had never really had a daddy. We went to dinner, and by noon the next day, he asked me to marry him. By 12:01, I had said yes, reminding him it was a package deal. He did not have a problem with that.

Renee got pregnant out of marriage while still living at home with her dad and me. It broke my heart, but I stood by her. She had a beautiful baby boy, and he became as important to me as the eyes in my head. It was not easy, at times, to feed an extra mouth, but by the grace of God, we never went hungry or had to sleep under a bridge. I was young, and whenever necessary, I was able to work two jobs to make ends meet.

Ragina supported her sister's pregnancy too, even after learning that she could not have children of her own. She didn't let jealousy get in the way of their friendship. Later, when Renee married and had kids, one after the other and five in all—John, Richard, Jessica, Dannielle, and Nicole—Ragina and I were there to help with the babies because, until meeting Tom[AP1], Renee was a bum magnet and hadn't ever had a real man to help her. We stuck together and made it through. As the children got older and started school, it was Ragina and I who helped buy school clothes for them.

Renee was so full of life and laughter. Anyone who knew her knew her laugh. She loved old people and children. Her house was where all the kids in town wanted to be. After all, she was just a big kid at heart and was able to relate to them. Her kids' friends would tell them, "I wish your mom was my mom. She is so great!" Renee also worked with the elderly, and whenever she had the opportunity, she would take in every stray she could, whether a kid or a dog. Luckily, she finally found and married Tom, who loved her enough to put up with the crowded house. Tom did his best as a dad, considering that when he married Renee, she already had four children and he had two. Renee was the happiest I had ever seen her when she was married to Tom. She loved him with all her heart, and I believe he loved her with all of his. Then again, no matter who you were, to know Renee *was* to love her.

Ragina, on the other hand, was the person you turned to whenever you needed to talk about something serious. I talked to her quite frequently about serious matters. She was more level-headed but still a lot of fun. Ragina married a man named Jay, and despite doctors saying she could never have kids, she became the mother of three miracle children—Sierra, Ann, and Dakota. Ragina had a beautiful singing voice. She led the worship team at her church and even had the opportunity to cut a solo album. I was so excited when I heard about it, because I knew it would be such a blessing to everyone who heard it.

Both girls were good mothers, good wives, and wonderful daughters. A mother could not have been more proud of her children than I was of mine. Even as they got older, it was always the three of us. They were my best friends. If I got up and it was storming, or even if the sun was bright in the sky, I would call the girls just to talk about the weather. We would talk about what we were going to have for dinner, trade recipes, or just laugh about some crazy thing we had seen on television that week. We were like the three musketeers. Each girl's husband would tell her, "You are just like your mother," to which we would all have a big laugh and say, "Well, of course. But who else better to be like?"

Ken and I lived in California until 1998, when I was asked to come to Spiro, Oklahoma, to pastor a church. After much prayer, I said yes, so we moved to Spiro, Oklahoma, to pastor the Lighthouse at the Crossroads church. I had never been away from my girls, but they were always supportive of my ministry. They had been raised in church. We talked on the phone two or three times a day and made at least two trips a year to California. The girls also made trips to Oklahoma.

Considering our bond, it was odd that the only good picture I had of the three of us together was when they were kids. That fact didn't dawn on me until Christmas of 2002. The girls had driven from California to Oklahoma so we could spend the holidays together. One day, we were shopping, and I was getting worn out. I told the girls I would just sit on a bench and wait until they were finished, but they said, "No way, Mom, you are not that old. You can keep up!" So I did.

During our browsing, I stopped at a one-hour photo shop. I told them I wanted to go in and have our picture taken because it had been years since the three of us had taken one together. They were worried about their hair and makeup but promised we would do it that summer when they came for their next visit. I agreed, not knowing that their next visit would never come.

Doomsday

Let that day be darkness;
let not God regard it from above,
neither let the light shine upon it.
—Job 3:4

It was July 16, 2003, a beautiful summer day. I knew that my two daughters, Ragina and Renee, and my six grandchildren, Richard, Jessica, Nikki, Sierra, Ann, and Dakota, were coming for a visit. I had already talked with them about three or four times that day. They were so excited about getting to my house.

We had so many plans. On Friday, we were going to Fort Smith, Arkansas, where Ragina was going to record her first solo CD. Then on the following week, we were going to Eureka Springs, Arkansas, where Ragina was going to sing at the Passion Play.

I was at the store getting groceries for everyone. After all, there were eight of them coming, and I wanted everything to be perfect. I called Ragina on my cell to ask what all the kids liked to drink and what kind of cereal to get. Renee, of course, wanted Dr. Pepper, and Ragina wanted Pepsi. I bought juice for all the little ones. While we were on the phone, Ragina informed me that she was going to do all of the cooking while she was here, and I told her that was fine with me. Then she told me what she wanted me to pick up for her, and I grabbed it all while I still had her on the phone. Then she passed the phone to Renee. Ragina was driving at this time so Renee could rest to drive later.

Renee was tired but really anxious to get here. She said it was really hot, and she wanted to know if the new pool would be ready to swim in by the time they got here. I assured her that it was being filled with water as we spoke. We had just bought a new swimming pool and had it installed before their visit so they could swim, have fun, and get relief from the summer heat.

Renee told me that they were at rest area in New Mexico and that Ragina was in the restroom. I asked her if they were all okay, and she said yes. Then she told me about an accident they had passed earlier that day.

"Mom," she said, "it was awful. A man was dead. His eyes were open, and he was looking at me."

"Oh my God!" I said. "See how fast things can happen?"

"I know, it was just awful."

I'm not sure if they had stopped at the accident or what, but one thing I knew for sure was this was so real to Renee that she was freaked out about it. Was it a premonition? I don't know. All I know is a few short hours later, it was my babies lying on the side of the road.

"Did you pray?"

"Yes."

We talked a little about how you never know what's going to happen to you on any given day and how it pays to constantly pray and know that everything is okay between you and God. Then I felt very compelled to tell her something.

"If you feel even so much as a bump in the road," I said, "you start praying. In fact, don't even wait until then. You start praying right now."

"Mom," she said, "I have been."

We laughed at me being such a worrywart, and then I told her I loved her.

"Be careful, and I will see you later tonight," I said. "Tell all the kids how much I love them, and tell Ragina I will talk to her later.

"I love you too, Mom," she said. And with that, we hung up.

At 6:30 that evening, on my way to church, I called the girls again see where they were. Ragina answered and told me they were just outside Amarillo, Texas. She sounded so tired, so I told her to stop in Amarillo and get a hotel room, and that I would pay for it with a credit card.

"No," she said. "Renee's been sleeping, so I'm going to pull over at the next stop and let her drive."

"I'm worried about you both," I said. "You sound too tired to be driving. I will call you after church and see where you're at.

She laughed. "We'll be home before you get out of church."

"If you got here that fast, it would be a miracle," I said, laughing in return.

At 8:45, church was over and I called Ragina's phone to check in. A man answered.

"What are you doing answering my daughter's phone?" I said.

"The people you are trying to get a hold of have been in an accident," he said.

"Oh my God. Those are my two daughters and my grandchildren. Are they okay?"

"That is what we are trying to find out. We have the police and ambulance on the way."

"Where are you?"

"Shamrock, Texas ..."

I heard sirens in the background, and then the phone went dead. My God, what should I do? I had to get home to Ken and let him know. We needed to find out if everyone was okay. I called Ragina's husband, Jay, and asked him if he had heard anything about the girls being in an accident.

"No," he said. "I just talked to Ragina, and everything was fine." I told him about my conversation with the man who had answered her phone, who, I later learned, was a truck driver who had seen the accident. Jay didn't seem to be very concerned. He just said he would call and see and call me back, which he never did.

I finally pulled into the driveway at home and rushed inside to tell Ken. We immediately jumped back in the car and started out for Shamrock. It would be about a six-hour drive from Spiro, Oklahoma, where we lived. I did not know if there was even a hospital there or if the kids would even need one, though the fact that neither of the girls answered the phone seemed a pretty good indicator they would.

We were just outside Oklahoma City when Renee's husband, Tom, called me on my cell phone.

"Thelma?" he said.

"Yes?"

"We lost Jessica, Renee, and Ragina."

I went numb. I expected him to just keep calling off names until everyone was gone, but he had stopped.

All I could think was, *No, no, no! What should I do? I can't tell Ken right now. He's driving. And Dannielle's in the backseat.* Dannielle was with us. It was her summer to spend with her grandfather and me.

How could I just blurt out something like that, right here and now, with absolutely no warning? How could I tell Ken that our daughters and beautiful sixteen-year-old granddaughter were gone, just like that? And how could I break it to Dannielle that she would never speak to her mom and sister (Renee and Jessica) again?

"How are the other kids?" I asked.

"They're being taken to Amarillo to the Northwest Texas Hospital. Everyone's okay except Ann. She's on life support."

My God. Not my five-year-old little beauty. This could not be happening to us. I hung up the phone and wondered again how I was going to break the news to Ken and Dannielle. I was afraid that Ken, after hearing my end of the conversation, might ask me what had happened, but luckily, he never did. Maybe he was too afraid to know the truth. Finally I had an idea. We were only a few miles from El Reno by then, and I had family there, so I asked Ken to stop at my cousin's house. Once we were all inside, I would break the news.

Now I just had to figure out how. How was I going to tell my husband that our daughters and granddaughter were just up and gone? How was I going to tell Dannielle that she would never hear her mom's voice again, let alone her aunt's and sister's? I still couldn't believe it myself. There had to have been a terrible mistake. I could not have just lost my children. Gone, just like that. No. I wouldn't believe it.

We were a good, Christian family. I was a pastor. Ragina was using her gift to sing to further God's kingdom, being on the praise and worship team at her church, and now releasing an album. Renee worked with the elderly and was wonderful with kids. We all tried our best to live according to God's will. So why was this happening to us?

And now we had seven grandchildren left and no mothers for any of them. This just couldn't be happening. Not to us. Not our family. This only happened to other people. It was something you read about happening to others and felt so bad about it, but so thankful, because all of your children and grandchildren were okay. What should I do? I couldn't fall apart. I had to hold up for all my grandchildren.

By the time we got to my cousin's house, I couldn't stand the pressure of not telling anymore. "Ken, we just lost our girls," I blurted out, tears streaming down my face.

My cousin Sharon was shocked. She said, "Thelma, are you sure?"

I said, "Yes, I'm sure." Ken was white. Dannielle was screaming.

Ken just fell up against the wall.

Dannielle began screaming, "I want my mom! I want my mom!"

Oh, God. I couldn't handle this. I wanted to scream too but knew I couldn't. Dannielle needed me right now.

So I said, "I want her too, baby, but we will get through this together." But I was thinking, *Get through it? My God, how can you ever get through losing a child and much less all your children at one time? God, what am I going to do?*

As I continued holding Dannielle, I wondered what could have happened. Had Renee fallen asleep at the wheel? No, she would not have taken a chance like that. If she'd have been that tired, she would have pulled over. And besides, Ragina said Renee had been sleeping all day. So what could have gone wrong? Sharon; her husband, Buster; and her sons, Roy and Steve, got into their car to follow us to Amarillo. Roy and Ragina were like brother and sister. Roy and the girls had been raised together.

My God, my babies are gone. And I still don't know how all the other grandchildren are. Please, God, let them be okay.

My phone rang. It was Jay.

"Thelma, Ann is still on life support, and she is bad. You need to get here as soon as possible."

Oh, my God, I can't take this too. Please keep Ann okay, I prayed silently.

It was morning by the time we arrived at Northwest Texas Hospital, and as I was getting out of the car, I was convinced that none of it was actually real. I was sure I would wake up and find out it was all a bad dream, or maybe it was just a cruel joke. The girls would drive up any minute now, and we would all have a big laugh at what a worrywart I am. Renee would laugh the most, because she always does. Ragina would say, "Mom, we're okay! Now where's all that Pepsi you bought? I need one."

But that is not what happened. Instead, Ken and I walked into the emergency room and told the lady at the desk that we were looking for our children who had been in a car accident in Shamrock the night before. Before I knew it, there were nurses and people all around us, and one nurse was holding me and helping me to an elevator. She was taking me to see the grandchildren.

My God, what would I say to them if they asked me about their moms and about Jessica? Did they know? God, please don't let any of them ask me. I have to wait until Jay and Tom can get here to tell them. My heart was going to burst. I wanted to die. But I couldn't. The children now had no one but me, as far as a woman in their lives.

The nurse led me out of the elevator and down the hallway into a room. There were Nikki and Sierra, both with their arms in slings and with bruises and cuts all over. All I could do was cry and ask them if they were all right. I felt like a zombie. I was walking and talking, but nothing was real. I was breathing in and out, but it wasn't me. It was as though I were watching it all happen to someone else. It was so sad to see so much pain.

I finally asked the girls where Ann was, and they told me she was still in the ICU. When I arrived in her room, I almost hit the floor. There was this beautiful little five-year-old girl, so frail, and with tubes coming out of every part of her. She was on a ventilator that was breathing for her, and I couldn't stand it. I felt like I was going to pass out. *Oh, God help me,* I prayed silently. *I have to be strong for all my grandchildren. I am the only woman left in their lives.*

Finally, I got the nerve to ask to see my daughters. But I couldn't. The reply when I asked was, "They are still in Shamrock, Texas. They never made it to the hospital but died on the side of that road."

It was real. My beautiful daughters were gone. It was only me. How could this be happening? It had always been the three of us. Jay and Tom arrived at the hospital the next morning. They wanted to tell the grandchildren about their mothers. It was so hard because Sierra kept asking for her mother. Nikki was still on so many meds that I don't think she even realized what had happened. Richard was in bad shape. He went into surgery right after we arrived at the hospital.

He asked me, "Where are Mom and Aunt Gina?" I guess the look on my face told the story. He said, "They died, didn't they, Grandma?"

I began to cry. He said, "How is Jessica?"

I said, "Baby, she is gone too."

We held each other and cried but decided it was best not to tell the other girls yet. Sierra came out of her room and asked the nurse, "Where is my mom?"

The nurse and I just looked at each other. Then the nurse said, "She is upstairs."

I guess in reality that was the truth. Thank God Richard, Nikki, and Sierra were out of the hospital in three days. Now we had to get them all back to California. Jay had Sherry, who was Ragina's best friend, come and fly back with Sierra. We still had to go to Shamrock to identify Ragina, Renee, and Jessica, so we took Richard and Nikki to the motel across the street. Ken and Tom went to Shamrock. Jay stayed at intensive care with Ann, and I stayed at the motel with Richard and Nikki.

All we knew at this time was that the back tire on the driver's side of the car had just separated. It was a Ford Excursion, so it was so big there was no way to control it. The police had told us that no matter who had been driving, they could not have controlled that car. They determined that Renee was not speeding. They were headed eastbound at the seventy-one mile marker when that car stopped rolling on a westbound access road. Everyone was thrown out except Renee and Dakota. Everyone was unconscious except Sierra, who was six years old. She saw everything and everyone. Richard was in the freeway, Nikki was on the side of the road, and Jessica had gone through the windshield. Ragina's seatbelt broke, and she was thrown out. (Oh God, help me get through this.) It took them a while to find Ragina because she was under the car. I was never allowed to see any of them. That's the hardest part because I didn't get to hold them and say good-bye. They were gone before we knew it. Only God knows why.

On that day, my sister, Wilma, my niece Charlotte, and my nephew Ron, who had flown in from California to help us get everyone back to California, flew back home with Richard and Nikki, who were both in wheelchairs. When we got to the Dallas airport, we were waiting on our next flight to Los Angles. People were looking at us and wondering what had happened. I could not talk to anyone, but Ron, who was my girls' pastor as well as their first cousin, was telling the lady at the ticket counter what happened. All I remember was looking at them. Then Charlotte joined them. The next thing I knew, everyone was crying. They put us in first class, and we boarded first. As people were getting on the plane, they would take time to say, "We are praying for you and your family."

There are so many wonderful people in the world, but all you hear on the news most of the time is about the bad. But here were strangers I had never seen before or since offering me comfort. It was like I was standing outside of myself watching this happen but it was not happening to me. Pastor Ron preached the funeral. We had them all at the same time, and they are buried right next to each other. It was the biggest funeral I have ever seen. People lined up for blocks trying to get

13

in. There were three overflow rooms with TVs, and still people were lined up for blocks up the street. The cemetery was so full that all you could see was people shoulder to shoulder. As I have said, Ragina was on the praise and worship team at Pastor Ron's church, and they had made a CD, so Ragina sang at her, her sister's, and her niece's funeral. No one else could have done a better job. My baby sang at her own funeral. My God, just to think of it now is almost more than my mind can bear. I always thought she would sing at mine.

What Now?

[S]eeing I have lost my children,
and am desolate, a captive ...
Behold, I was left alone.
—Isaiah 49:21

What were my seven remaining grandchildren going to do now that none of them had a mother to guide them? All of them had lost a mother and an aunt, and in Jessica, a sister or a cousin. None of them would ever be the same. Their lives were changed forever.

Jay, Ragina's husband, didn't even believe in God, so how would her children be brought up the way she wanted? All three of them—Sierra, Ann, and Dakota—had been in church since they were conceived. Now they would be in the control of Jay, a self-proclaimed atheist who thought you could live anyway you wanted because when this life was over, it's over. If only he knew Ragina was still very much alive and well in God's arms and would always live on, because we all were made to be eternal.

Dakota would not even remember his mother and how she loved him so much. He wouldn't remember how she held him, cared for him, and sat up with him when he was sick. He wouldn't remember how she played with him and what she taught him. Yes, he still had a wonderful dad, but he would never get the chance to really know his mother. And the memories that Sierra and Ann had of the accident would be with them the rest of their lives.

Jay would probably remarry, and there would be nothing wrong with that. But these children would never have their real mother back, and I could only hope that any stepmother Jay chose for them would love them and not mistreat them in the way you hear about so many times in the news. *God, please help my grandchildren to go on to have some type of normal life!*

And as for Renee's five children—my God, they lost everything when they lost their mother because she was all they had as far as a real parent. That was not to take anything away from Tom, because he did his best. I loved Tom. But so far, it seemed as if we'd lost him too. He just was not himself after the accident, and on top of that, he was now drinking a lot.

I took in Renee's remaining two girls, Dannielle and Nicole, or Danni and Nikki, as we called them. Dani had already been living with us, and now that Jessica was gone, Nikki wanted to be here with the only sister she had left. We legally adopted both Dannielle and Nikki. We told them they could keep their last name if that's what they wanted. But both of them said they wanted the Wehunt name. Dannielle has her mom's name as her middle name—Dannielle Renee—and Nikki was Nicole Breann. Nikki wanted her aunt Gina's name. I had second thoughts but gave in to her changing her name to Ragina Nicole. I told her she had always been Nikki and that was what she was still to go by, so that was okay. But hindsight, that was a mistake. Always go with your first instinct.

Nikki continued living with Tom until September 2003. Danni and I had gone to California that month for a memorial jump that a group of skydivers were giving in Ragina's honor, and when we left, Nikki came home with us.

I didn't bring the girls to live with me to hurt Tom, although for some reason, I suspect it did. I brought them here because they wanted to be here, and they were already going through enough pain. I didn't want to add to it by saying no. I felt it was what was best for them. God help me if it was a mistake. I was just trying to make it one day at a time.

If only it had been me who had died in that crash. Then everyone else could have made it just fine. My two girls and their husbands would still have their children, and the children would still have their mothers. But as it is, everyone's lives were messed up forever. Ragina's beautiful voice was silenced, along with Renee's wonderful zest for life and her beautiful laugh.

What had gone wrong? Was it me? Was God punishing me for something? I knew I was far from perfect, but I did the best I could. What was it? Why were so many of them taken at one time, and why all of my children? It wasn't fair. I was going to grow old with no children to lean on or talk to.

I felt like such a failure. I kept thinking that there must have been something I could have done to keep it all from happening. I had prayed for them all day on the day they were killed, and it still didn't stop that terrible accident from happening. For a long time, that idea made me afraid to pray, because I thought that when I prayed, people would die. It also made me angry at God. Where had he been in all this? What was he thinking? I wasn't Job—I couldn't lose all my children at once!

"God, what have I done to deserve this?" I often prayed. "I know I have made a lot of mistakes in my life, but for the last nine years, I have devoted my life to your work. I even left all my family to follow you. So what is going on here? Please give me an answer I can understand. I know you are a just God and that nothing you do is a mistake, but this … this sure seems like one big mistake to me."

It was so unfair. In Ragina and Renee, I had lost not just my only living children but my best friends. I missed them more than life. I could not stop thinking about that last Christmas we spent together shopping, and how now I would never have a picture of the three of us together with them fully grown.

Part II

The Long, Dark Tunnel

Numb

Let the day perish wherein I was born
—Job 3:3

It had been seven months since the accident. I remembered when Daddy went to be with Jesus. For about three years after that, I was just angry. But this time was different. Sometimes, I was angry, but mostly I was just lost. And numb. And then I would get these moments where all I wanted to do was cry and then run. But none of those things would have really made a difference. The bottom line was always the same: my babies were gone, and I was left here.

I had heard people say, "It will get better," and I thought that by now, the pain would at least be starting to let up. But it was only getting worse.

Too frequently, it was all I could do just to get out of bed. And then when I did, I would walk straight to the living room and look at the girls' pictures. Sometimes as I looked at them, I'd feel nothing. Just numb. Other times, I'd pick up their pictures and give them each a big good-morning kiss. And then there were those times that I'd see them and feel this intense, burning anger.

The rest of the day, I'd find myself sitting in a chair and not even getting dressed or combing my hair. I'd sit and think about what I had lost and could never get back. I rarely took care of the house. Sometimes I'd feel so tired and physically sick that I was sure I couldn't go on another minute, at which point all I wanted to do was give up and go die alone. And on those rare occasions when I got myself out of the house, I'd often be driving down the road when, suddenly, it was like a sledgehammer had hit me in the gut and I'd just want to lie down and die. Wednesday nights were the worst. I'd always feel a sick to my stomach on the way home from church—probably because it was a Wednesday night when the girls had the accident.

These were the times other people never saw; only God knew what was going on. It was all I could do in those days just to keep going. I figured if my body got tired enough, it would shut down on its own. My mind was already doing that on a regular basis. Whenever I just couldn't cope anymore, my mind would go into some kind of limbo I couldn't explain. I guess it was God's way of protecting me so that when someone or something needed my attention, I could at least be physically present to give it.

My doctors offered me all kinds of tranquilizers, but I knew that was not the answer. As soon as the drugs wore off, I would still have to face the fact that my children were gone. Plus, my grandchildren had already lost so much. I was not going to also let them lose their grandmother to a bottle of pills.

I would have not made it through most days had it not been for God's protection and Ken's strength.

Ken and I had met in the fourth grade. Our parents were friends, and both of our dads were ministers. What a pair we were. I didn't like Ken when we were kids. He went the way of rebellion and I the way of the straight and narrow. I loved the Lord and singing his praises in church while Ken hated even going to church. He was not my type at all. And yet here I was married to him. Our marriage had not always been an easy road because he had issues with anger and bitterness, but deep down, he had a heart of gold.

And now, he was a rock to me. Whenever I couldn't focus or do the things I needed to, Ken stepped up and kept things going as well as he could. It was Ken who kept everything livable. He took Danni and Nikki where they needed to go and did all the shopping. It must have been very hard on him, although, at the time, I was so absorbed in my pain that I didn't even realize it. It was getting to the point where I didn't want to get out of bed—ever. But I had no choice.

"The kids will be up soon, and they'll need me," I'd say every morning, just to get myself up.

Loving and caring for the grandchildren and knowing how much they needed me was what kept me going. When Nikki had first come to live with us, she was having a lot of panic attacks and not sleeping well, and she said she kept seeing the accident in her mind over and over again. We prayed a lot together, and by the grace of God, the attacks started lessening. The good thing about Nikki was that she was able to talk about her pain and ask questions. She and I would cry together and get mad together, and it helped us both to be able to do that.

One night, when Nikki and I were driving home from church, we hit a really rough spot in the road, and Nikki said to me, "Grandma, you don't like to drive over rough roads, do you?"

I said, "No, it tears up the car. And it's very uncomfortable."

About that time, we drove onto a new section of road, and Nikki said, "See, Grandma? Now we are on a smooth part of the road."

"Okay," I said. "What are you saying?"

"Well, losing mom and Jessica and Aunt Gina was our rough road. But someday it will smooth out and be better."

I thought, *My God, what wonderful wisdom from a child.* And then I remembered the verse in the Bible that said we must become as humble as little children.

"Grandma?" she went on. "God never takes anything without giving something back, does he?"

I smiled. "No, baby, he doesn't."

"So, he took mom and Aunt Gina and Jessica—or at least he allowed them to be taken from us—but then God gave you to me and Dannielle. And he gave me and Dannielle to you.

"Yes, he did, and I thank God for giving us to each other," I said.

Despite her wisdom, though, Nikki continued having the nightmares and panic attacks, and I just never knew what to do to help her. All I could do when each incident arose was to be there and to hold her.

But who was holding me?

As not only the sole woman in my grandchildren's lives but also the minister of my church, I felt it my duty to comfort everyone else. But I didn't feel strong enough. I was never sure how to respond when people said to me, "You are such a strong person. I don't know how you do it." I wanted to tell them, "You don't know what it is really like when I am alone."

I tried to say and do all of the "right" things when I was in front of other people, but on the inside, I was dead. I had died on the side of Interstate 40 that July evening in 2003, along with my daughters and granddaughter. Now I was just a shell of a human, trying to put one foot in front of the other, breathing in and out, just making it through the day until I could go to bed and get up the next morning to do it all over again.

Too many days, I wondered how long I could go on like this, with this terrible pain in my heart but trying to be strong. I just wanted the pain to go away, but I knew it would never happen. Not until I could go and be with my girls again. Several times, I'd find myself praying, *Oh, God, please send Jesus down to get us so we can all be together again!*

To boot, I found myself being more and more worried about Dannielle, who handled things a lot differently than Nikki. Her whole personality had changed. She was hard, like nothing bothered her. I knew it was because she was hurting, but she would not talk about it. Whenever I'd ask her how she was, she'd act like everything was okay. She was angry all the time too and had started doing things that were not normal for her. She was being drawn to the wrong type of kids, for example, and even after I prohibited her from socializing with certain people, she continued talking to them anyway. And then, as if that weren't enough, to cover it up, she began lying to me about who she was hanging out with or on the phone with. She was a good girl, and I knew that, but I was worried about her behavior and the fact that she wouldn't talk to me about anything.

By the time I legally adopted the girls, Nikki was twelve and Danni was thirteen, a very difficult age range in the best of times, much less in this period of pain and grief. On the day the adoption was final, Nikki said to me, "See, Grandma, God took two people away from you, but now he's given you two back." I just held her and we cried. Tom had never adopted them or had any kind legal custody. Their real dad was on drugs and drank like a fish, and the girls were afraid he would try to get them.

There was no question about it: I was blessed to have Dannielle and Nikki. So it seemed particularly unfortunate that, with the extra mouths to feed, we now found ourselves unable to keep up with the bills. And no one was stepping up to help us. The clothes, the food, the cell phones—how would we ever keep up? I could see and feel the worry in Ken. He was almost to the end of his rope.

But what would I do if anything happened to him? I could never make it on my own.

Forever Changed

Though I speak, my grief is not asswaged:
and though I forbear, what am I eased?
—Job 16:6

For the first time since the accident, Ken and I went out without Danni and Nikki. We went out to eat with some friends of ours, Joann and Jerry. I felt so guilty leaving the girls at home alone. I felt like I was leaving them out, and it made me very uncomfortable. Joann and I were like sisters. We had worked in the ministry together for about twenty years, and she was a great blessing in the ministry. I told Ken one time, "I hope I never have to choose between you and Joann, because she is a much better singer." I don't know what I would have done without her.

I asked Ken, "Why do I feel so guilty going out without the girls?"

He didn't have an answer. It was just so hard to always know the right thing to do, and I often second-guessed myself. I felt so lost. These were things that I would have normally asked Renee and Ragina about, but they, of course, were not here. If only I could still be just Grandma and not Mom again. It was so unfair, to me and to these girls. They needed their mom and their Aunt Gina, not to mention their older sister, Jessica, whom they looked up to so much.

Before Ken and I had left the house, we'd ordered and brought home pizza for the girls. They hadn't seemed to mind that we were going, but I still was not comfortable with it.

We had only been gone a little while when Nikki called and asked if they could go to the movies with some friends. I knew the kids they were going with and trusted them. Plus, Nikki told me that Ricky would be driving, and about five of the other kids from the church would be with them, so I said okay. In fact, I was really glad they had asked the girls to go. At least now I didn't feel quite so guilty; for a while, I could quit thinking about them just sitting at home, alone and unsupervised. I was glad they were making friends here.

When we got home that night, we had a breakthrough with Dannielle. Ken came out of her room and told me she was in there crying. When I went in to check on her, she was lying on her bed with her back toward the door. I sat down on the bed next to her.

"What's wrong?" I asked.

"Nothing."

"Grandma can't help you if you don't talk to me," I said.

"I said nothing is wrong."

I knew better, but I said, "Okay. Well, are you just having a bad day? Like Grandma does at times?"

"Yes."

"Are you missing your mom and sister and Aunt Gina?" I probed deeper.

She started to cry harder, and then, through the sobs, I heard a muffled yes.

"It's okay to cry," I told her. "And it is okay to miss your mom, and your sister and aunt."

Finally, she sat up, and we held each other and cried together.

That night, I was able to release some of the tension I had been carrying around. I had been so worried about Dannielle suppressing her feelings about what had happened to all of us. Losing Ragina, Renee, and Jessica had changed all of our lives forever, and we couldn't pretend that it hadn't. Problem was, I felt that nothing would ever be all right again.

I'm Not Job!

I am weary with my groaning;
all the night make I my bed to swim;
I water my couch with my tears.
—Psalm 6:6

*I*t had been almost a year since the accident, and now John, Nikki and Dani's brother, was moving from California to live with us. When he came, he brought his girlfriend, whose name was also Danielle but spelled with only one *n*. And that wasn't all. The two announced that they were going to get married.

I wanted to be happier for them than I was, but I felt too burdened by the real-life circumstances surrounding the whole situation. They were too young, for one, although I knew both had been forced to grow up fast.

Second, of course, the two of them wanted to stay with us until they could get enough money to live on their own. John said he planned to get a job and would use his money to save enough to buy them a house.

Finally, it just seemed so unfair that Renee could not be there to see her first son be married—or to see any of her children be married, for that matter. Ragina would've been such a big help with the wedding too. She had helped raise both John and Richard, and they'd been like sons to her.

But as it was, Danielle's mother was not here. She was in California and was no help even in raising Danielle. Danielle's dad and stepmom had raised her, and Danielle never got along with her stepmom, which put a lot of strain on her relationship with her dad. Of course, Renee was in heaven. There was no one who would step up and help me shoulder the responsibility. I alone would have to be the one to take them in and help them until they could make it on their own.

I wondered how other mothers my age made it after losing their children. Did they have to take care of their grandchildren this way? All I knew was that, somehow, God had to help me work it all out, because there was no way I could do it all alone.

Now that John was here, Richard was the only one of Renee's kids still at home. I missed Richard so much, and I worried about him. I knew Tom loved him, but right now, Tom couldn't even take care of himself. In fact, Richard had recently told me on the phone that Tom was gone about twenty hours a day. That meant the boy was on his own for most of the time, with no supervision, and he was only sixteen. That was an age when boys really needed to be supervised and led in the right direction.

From what he and John had told me, he seemed okay, but how could he be when he was basically left to raise himself? Should I try to make him come out to live with us too? I still wasn't sure that was the right thing to do. He was sixteen, and if he didn't want to come out, I was not going to make him.

* * *

I have church tonight and I have a splitting headache, was all I could think. It was about 4:00 p.m., and for the past hour or so, I had been just sitting, wondering what we were going to do about money. My checking account was almost two hundred dollars overdrawn, and I couldn't figure out what I had done wrong. I must have overlooked something.

It didn't help that Nikki had run our cell phone bill up to almost a thousand dollars that month. I had no choice but to pay it. Now I was wondering how I was going to pay all of the other bills. All we were living on by this time were our retirement checks and my salary from the church. For a while now, Ken had been picking up odd jobs here and there, but this week there had been nothing, and it was really hurting us.

Renee was a stay-at-home mom who hadn't built up much Social Security income, so all there was to be divided among the children was about $275 per month. I think they got about $74 each a month. Thank God for the church people who had businesses. They gave Ken and me odd jobs. I would do some paperwork for Robert Cooper, and William took Ken on jobs with him, but with but with four extra people to feed and clothe, that didn't go far. The people at the church were wonderful, and the salary was wonderful until our family grew overnight. Then when I felt I could no longer do the church or God justice, for the sake of the people, decided I had to resign. That but a huge hole in our finances, but I still felt like it was the right thing to do. I wasn't there for the money; I was there to do my best for God and the people.

I'd never realized how much it cost to raise children in this day, and we had four of them. The grocery bill alone had tripled, and we were looking at almost a thousand dollars a month. And next year, they were all going to start back to school, which meant more clothes and lunch money and all of the extras. How did people do it?

Of course, the kids thought we were made out of money, because before the accident, whenever they had wanted something, we just sent it to them. What they didn't realize was that it was different now. Back then, we had just been Grandma and Grandpa. We hadn't had to provide for all of them on a daily basis; we had just done the fun stuff. Food and housing were taken care of by their parents.

For instance, if we were still just Grandma and Grandpa, we could have helped John and Danielle in their efforts to get their own house, like we really wanted to. John had gotten a job and was trying to save all of his paychecks, but we were in no shape to help them. And to top it off, we hadn't been able to get John's check earlier that week because he was on the account with his grandpa, and Ken was gone. I had suggested that my name be put on it as well, since I was always there, even when the two of them were not. When John got a job, he wanted his own account, but because he was not eighteen, he had to have an adult on the account. John had found a job at a sod company putting down sod at homes, so it was a bit of a help because at least he could help himself and his little family. It was not enough to fully support a family, but I was thanking God for any kind of help.

John said no to me being on his account, though, which really hurt my feelings. It made me feel as though he was afraid I would take something from him. My God, it was spring, and he and Danielle had been at our house since January. In that time, I had never asked him for so much as a dime, even though he was working, and believe me, we could have used the help. I had never asked any of my kids or grandkids for anything ever, and I had done more for that child than anyone in his life had ever done for him. Talk about adding insult to injury.

God, what are we going to do? I silently prayed.

Apparently, it was time to scale back to the basics. If we could just make ends meet well enough to pay for the house and car, and to buy food, that would at least keep them warm and fed. I hated this. It stunk. But there was nothing I could do to change it. I loved my grandchildren, and there was nothing I wouldn't do to take care of them. They were wonderful kids who made my life worth living.

I opened my Bible and read portions from the book of Job. He had lost all of his children and everything he'd owned, and still kept his faith in God. My life undoubtedly seemed to be going in the same direction as his, except for one thing—I was no Job! I had not lost my faith in God. In fact, my faith was what often got me through the day—but right now, I couldn't help wondering where God was in the midst of this storm.

God, why couldn't you have taken me instead of my girls? I don't want to be here. I can't do this. I'm not as strong as people say. God, please forgive me for being so weak, but I am no Job!

Finally, I talked it over with Ken, and we decided to sell our fishing home on Lake Eufala about forty miles from were we lived. It was a beautiful little two-bedroom rock cabin. It was only one bedroom when we bought it, and Ken had built on the other bedroom. And we had an acre of land next to us we could also sell. The cabin had been Ken's retreat—a place where he could just get away and relax. But you do what you have to. And to us, what mattered most was the grandchildren.

Pain Squared

So went Satan forth …
and smote Job with sore boils
from the sole of his foot unto his crown.
—Job 2:7

Easter came and went. It was okay, but it didn't seem any different than any other day. One day seemed to just run into another, and nothing made any sense anymore. At least I got to talk to Ragina's family from California—my other grandkids, Sierra, Ann, and Dakota, and my son-in-law, Jay. They had called to tell me Happy Easter, and they seemed to be doing well. The kids sounded as okay as they could under the circumstances, although Jay said Sierra was beginning to act out.

I wished he would let the kids come out that summer and spend some time with us. I thought it would do them good to spend time with Danni, Nikki, and John, since all of the cousins had been such a big part of one another's lives before the accident. Now it must have seemed to them that they had lost everything—not just their mom and aunt and cousin, but all of their cousins, who were also their good friends. If only Jay could see that, he might let them stay longer. He'd said he would bring them out to see us eventually, but I wanted him to bring them out and let them stay with us, and then I would take them back home later.

A few days after Easter, I was having physical symptoms that got me admitted to the hospital. At first I thought I was having a heart attack. The pain in my chest was so terrible. Ken drove me to the hospital. No one knew what was wrong, so the doctors had me stay and did all kinds of tests. The tests showed that I had pancreatitis. Then, three days later,

31

I broke out with shingles. My God, I had never had so much pain in my life. The doctor said it was caused by nerves. Go figure. Just when I thought I had been handling things pretty well, my body was telling me a different story. The boils began to come around my body and down my left side into the groin area and down the inside of my leg. Death would have been a relief, but that was not to be. The doctor had came in and told me this was a life-threatening case of the shingles and that he had never seen shingles as bad in his time as a doctor. Oh well, leave it to me to make history.

I wasn't able to leave the hospital for an entire month, and after being discharged, I was still in a lot of pain. The doctors and nurses had told me the pain could last a long time and that sometimes it never went away. That made me a nervous wreck. I was already planning to live in emotional pain for the rest of my life. I didn't think I could take it to be in physical pain forever too. Luckily, though, the pain did subside—at least most of it. And luckily, through the whole ordeal, Ken was wonderful, taking care of me and the girls and the house. I don't know how he did it.

I had to trade in my truck for a car, however, because, even though the pain was less than it had been, it was too hard for me to climb up into the truck. I was able to trade in for a black Chrysler 300 C, but the thrill and the joy of getting a new car was not there like it would have been had my Ragina and Renee still been with me. I had shared everything with my girls, and now nothing really excited me because I didn't have them to share it with. Nothing had any meaning, including this. It was just a car.

I imagined that if they were there, Ragina would love it because black was her favorite color, and Renee would be excited just because she was an excited girl, and she loved new things and loved life. She would have wanted to drive it everywhere too, and that would have been okay with me.

Danni and Nikki were there, though, and they were excited, which gave me a smile. Danni was so much like her mother. I thanked God the girls were in my life. I would have died without them. I hoped they were glad that I was in their lives as well. It did seem as though we were all a comfort to one another. Some of the time, at least; remember, they were teenagers.

In the ensuing weeks, however, Nikki got into a mood. When I asked her about it, she said she was just missing her brothers. I knew she was, but I couldn't help but feel that it also had something to do with the fact that she had just broken up with her boyfriend. She had done the right thing; he had been playing her. He'd ask her out, she'd say yes, and then he wouldn't show up or answer his phone when she called. But if I told her he was playing her, just asking her out just to see if she would say yes and then laughing behind her back, she only got mad at me. I just had to play it right and be there for her, even when she thought I wasn't. It was hard at my age not to try to shield her from all of the hurt. I had been a teenager and raised two teenagers—one of them her mother—so I could see what was going to happen before it did. I knew that the game was the same and that only the players had changed. But I knew I couldn't interfere. All that would do was ruin the relationship Nikki and I had, because she wouldn't listen to me anyway. I thanked God that I had peace at least over this one matter. I only wished Ken felt the same. He wanted to be Hitler and rule it all, but I told him that would never help in raising teenagers today; it hadn't even helped when we were teenagers.

Unfortunately, however, the small bit of peace I had would not last for long, for nearly two years after losing my daughters and beautiful granddaughter, I also lost my mother. I booked a flight to California for the funeral, but when the day came to leave, I could not get on that plane. I was not emotionally able to face that funeral. It would mean seeing my mother, my father, my two daughters, and my granddaughter all in the same place, and I just couldn't do it. All I'd had was in that cemetery, and I could not face it. I felt like a coward.

Part III

Going Deeper:
Life on the Home Front

Sierra

Depart from me, all ye workers of iniquity;
for the LORD hath heard the voice of my weeping.
—Psalm 6:8

Jay remarried, and he was no longer the same person. He had already changed after the accident; it had been almost like he had died with Ragina. But now that he was remarried, I didn't know the man anymore. Suddenly, he was not letting me see or talk to the kids, and I had done nothing to him that I was aware of. I hadn't said or done anything differently than normal, and when I'd met his new wife, Lori, on the phone, I had been very respectful to her and very supportive of the new marriage.

Of course, I couldn't help wondering what role Sue had in Jay's new demeanor. I had first met her when she and Jay were just engaged, and she had seemed to be a very decent and caring person. But as soon as they had gotten married, Jay changed so much that I had to wonder about her involvement in it.

Then one day, despite him not letting me talk to the kids, I managed to speak to Ann, since when I called, she answered and then didn't tell her dad who it was. Jay must not have been within earshot, because she went on to tell me that he and her new mom had locked Sierra in the garage the day before and that, starting today, Sierra no longer lived with them.

My mind reeled, but I didn't ask any questions. Instead, I just asked her to put her dad on the phone.

Jay answered but seemed distant. I asked him if he was okay and whether I had done anything wrong; I wanted to make sure we were on decent terms before trying to have a conversation with him.

As soon as he said no, I got down to business.

"Tell me where Sierra is," I said.

"You can't talk to her," he said.

"Why?"

There was a pause, and then he began to sob. Finally, he managed to say, "In time ..."

"What the hell does that mean?" I said. "What have you done to Sierra?"

This was not like Jay. What was going on, and why was Sierra suddenly the target? I immediately hung up and called a private investigator. I had to get to the bottom of this, and most of all, I had to find Sierra. At the very least, I had to know she was okay.

It didn't take long. The PI found Sierra back home in California but said she had been in Oregon at Jay's mom's house. Why hadn't he just told me? All of this anger and worry could have been avoided. And what about all of this business about her being locked in the closet? Why would Ann have said that Sierra wasn't going to live with them anymore if Jay and Sue had only intended to send Sierra away to his mom's house temporarily? Something didn't wash.

So I called another attorney and explained what had happened, and I told him I wanted visitation rights to see my grandchildren. He agreed to take my case.

A few days before our court case in California, I packed my bags and headed to the airport. I hadn't even told Jay I was coming because I knew he'd do all he could to keep the kids from seeing me. Instead, I had arranged for my sister Wilma and her son Ron to pick me up at the airport and then take me by the school to see the girls. Assuming there were no delays at the airport, we'd get to the school just as the kids were being dismissed for the day. I felt bad sneaking around like that, but I knew it was the only way I'd get to see my grandkids—and I had to see them.

We arrived at 2:40, just in time to hear the final school bell ring. Now all I had to do was wait until the girls come out. My heart was beating so fast! Finally, here came Sierra, and as soon as she saw me, she began running and screaming, "Grandma! It's my Grandma!" She reached me, jumped into my arms, and held onto me so tightly. I knew she didn't understand my tears as I told her how much I loved her.

After a moment, she pulled away and started looking around. Just then, Ann walked up, and Sierra ran to her, saying, "Ann, it's Grandma Thelma! It's Grandma Thelma, Ann!"

Ann leaped into my arms and gave me my second tight squeeze. It felt so good to hold my granddaughters again. Couldn't Jay see what he was doing to these kids by keeping them away from me? They loved me, and I loved them.

The girls asked me to walk them home from school, and I said yes. I wasn't sure what would happen when we got there, but whatever it was, it wasn't these kids' fault—so I wasn't going to take it out on them and say no.

On our way back, Sierra asked me if I'd come in to see Dakota when we got there, and all I could say is, "I don't know, baby, we will see. I'm not sure if I can come in or not."

She looked at me inquisitively. "But why not? You are our grandma."

"I know, baby, but we will just have to see," I said and then changed the subject to something positive, telling them how much I loved them and had missed them.

When we got to the house, Sierra ran inside, so excited, saying, "My grandma is here, my grandma is here!"

I stayed standing outside the front door, and Sue came to the door, saying, "Yep, that's your grandma," all the while blocking the doorway with her arms across it, as if she thought I would try to barge in. Obviously, I was not welcome.

"You're not to see Sierra," was all she said after that.

"Tell Jay he is going to talk to me, one way or the other," was my only reply, although I wanted to say a lot more.

"Sierra's fine. She has not suffered anything," she said.

What kind of a response was that? I hadn't said a word about Sierra suffering, so why was she suddenly bringing that up? And why was Sue only concerned that I not see Sierra? What about the other grandkids? Besides, Sue was crazy if she thought Sierra hadn't suffered anything. Sierra was the only grandchild who had had not been unconscious at some point during the accident, which meant her mother, her aunt, and her cousin had died right before her eyes. It also meant that Sierra had seen her sister be taken away in a helicopter and the rest of the kids put into ambulances. And that wasn't to say anything about the horror stories that I had heard from the kids since Sue had entered the picture.

Stories about Sierra being put into the bathroom overnight and having to sleep on the hard floor. Stories about her being locked in the garage and being told she was bad and that bad girls got "sent away." And worst of all, stories about how Jay had hosed her down in front of his drunk friends and then said Sierra's counselor had told him to do it for punishment. There was no other way to say it: this woman was stupid if she thought Sierra had suffered nothing. My God, what was going on here? I had nothing more to say to this woman, so I just walked away. Wilma had followed me in her car and was at the curb, so I got in her car and went to stay with her. That's were I was when Jay called.

Later, Jay called me and said he would meet me at the park at 8:00 p.m.

"Just make sure you're alone," he said.

"Fine. No problem." Had I known what was ahead of me, I would never have been so agreeable.

Wilma drove me to the park and waited for me in the car. When I arrived at the spot we'd agreed upon at a few minutes till 8:00, shock of shocks, Sue was also there as Jay's chaperone. Apparently Jay couldn't speak for himself anymore; he needed a mouthpiece. Although when I looked at him, I remembered why; these days, he was too drunk to ever speak for himself. If I followed my heart, I would have left right then, but I knew I would not be able to see the kids if I did, and that's what this was all about.

Sue made it plain that she would talk first, although I couldn't understand what she'd have to say, as these were not her children. This battle was between Jay and me, and although she might not realize that, I knew he did. Still, all we could do was let her talk and talk and talk. I knew it might be awhile, so I took a seat on the park bench.

I wasn't sure who she was trying to convince with all of her babble about how wonderful she was and how God had put her into these kids' lives. God would never send anyone into a child's life to abuse him. She went on about how sad it was that Jay couldn't drink anymore than he already did, at which point I thought, *Well, God help him if he does, because he can hardly stand as it is.* I knew Jay had been devastated when he'd lost Ragina or I thought he had and was just been trying to replace her—but this?

Finally, I had heard all I could take. I stood up, looked her in the eye, and said, "You will never break Sierra. She is her mother's daughter, and she will not be broken."

I turned to walk away when I got a sudden sharp pain in my head. My God, what was that? I fell to the ground. What was happening to me? The next thing I knew, Wilma was there trying to get Jay to help her lift me up. But he and Sue just stood there looking at me lying on the ground in pain. Then they walked around me, went to their car, and left. They went home and called the police on me.

God, help me. Am I having a stroke or what? Wilma couldn't get me up off the ground. *Please, God, give me the strength to get up!* I told her not to call 911 and that I would be okay, after which, somehow, I found the strength to get up, and Wilma helped me to the car.

From the park, she drove me directly to Pastor Ron's. Ron is my nephew, but more than that he was Ragina and Renee's pastor as well as their first cousin. He is a man of faith, and I knew prayer was the only thing that would help in this situation. I nearly fell into Pastor Ron's arms, and he prayed for me and told me that everything was going to work out. I knew he was telling me the truth. God would not allow this to go on. We visited for a while, and then Wilma's husband called and said the police had called looking for me.

So we headed to Wilma's house, where I called the police and told them I was there. The person on the other end said the police needed to talk to me and told me that an officer was on his way.

A few minutes later, I answered the door and introduced myself, after which the officer came in and immediately said he had a complaint against me from Jay Smith. I was stunned. What did I do? Here, Jay and Sue were the ones giving me hell, and they had a complaint against me!

"What's the complaint about?" I asked him.

"They told me you came all the way from Oklahoma to run off with their children."

My God, Jay really had lost his mind. What was going on with him? Was this just grief or guilt? Personally I go for the guilt, but in order to feel guilt, I think you have to have a heart. I would have helped a stranger in the shape I was in, but he and Sue were able to look at me on the ground and walk off, not knowing if I was having a stroke. Something really wrong had happened to him. Jay had never been a mean or hateful person. Whatever it was, he was definitely not himself.

Then again, what if he was being himself and I just hadn't ever known the real Jay? Ragina had loved him so much; maybe she had been keeping things about him from me and her dad. I just couldn't believe that was the case, though. After twelve years, Ken and I would have been able to see it—and we had never suspected a thing.

The holidays were coming again. I wished I could run away until they were over. No one knew what this time of year did to me, and sometimes I thought no one cared, as long as I stayed focused and took care of everything for them. This year was particularly bad because of money. We didn't even have enough to buy a Thanksgiving ham. Yet I was expected to just smile and act as if everything were normal.

God, what should I do? I know you have not put me out on this limb just to cut it off behind me, but I feel so helpless, and the girls don't understand. After all, Grandma has always been able to get them what they wanted. But that was when their mom was alive and all I had to be was the loving, generous grandmother.

It was with such prayers and God's help that we made it through Thanksgiving Day, and it was a good day. God provided everything we needed and more. Now all I had to think about was Christmas, but I knew God would work that out too.

I really wanted to have Sierra, Ann, and Dakota with us for at least part of the holiday, although I knew I shouldn't get my hopes up. I called their house, expecting Sue to answer and then refuse to give Jay the phone, but miracle of miracles, it was Jay's voice that I heard on the other line. I asked him if we could have the kids for part of the Christmas holiday if we came and picked them up and then brought them back home. He said he would think about it, which was a more hopeful response than I'd expected. I was smiling when I hung up.

About a week later, I was getting ready for church when my phone rang, and another miracle happened. It was Jay. He said we could come and get the kids on December 16 but that we had to promise to bring them back home by the twenty-third. I was so happy. I hung up the phone and thanked God for this Christmas miracle. I could hardly wait to spend time with those precious kids in my own home again, like we'd always used to. I would get to watch their excitement as they opened Christmas presents again. I would take so many pictures.

And then we got more news. My car was to be repossessed, and I knew our truck would be next without a miracle. Three weeks before, I had contacted a place that loans money to people awaiting for the wrongful death lawsuit settlements. From Ford motor Co. and Cooper Tires for negligence. They told me then that I would receive the money in approximately two days, and everything had seemed fine. But here it was now, almost a month later, and we still had no money. And now my car was gone. It was par for the course. The holidays of the last few years had been a nightmare at best, but now … there also would be no gifts under the tree. All my grandkids would be here, and I would not have a present for one of them. I had no choice but to look for the blessings amid the bad: at least we got to have Sierra, Ann, and Dakota for the week.

On the fifteenth, Ken and I and the girls drove the truck to California. Jay brought the kids to the hotel we were staying at, which I was relieved about, as I'd been a little worried about how we'd get past Lori, the gatekeeper. This way we didn't have to see her at all.

As soon as I heard the knock on our room door, I ran out of the room to meet them. I even hugged Jay and told him that I was not his enemy, and I meant it with all my heart. Jay hugged me tightly in reply. I knew he could feel my and Ken's love for him, and it just made my heart ache worse and my mind wonder even more how he could let a woman control him to the point that it was hurting his children. How could he not see she was up to? It was all about the money, and everyone in Taft knew it except Jay. Jay had a very high-paying job, and as soon as Sue read about Ragina's death, Sue set out to get him. Taft is where my girls were born and raised most of their lives. It was a small town, and everyone knows everyone. I didn't even want to think about what Sue would do if she got her hands on these children legally. I just had to be there for Jay and the children. Even though I didn't agree with everything Jay was doing, he was the father of my grandchildren, and I would stand behind him if he ever needed me.

The kids' stay with us was such a blessing, although—for me, at least—it was still mixed with heartache. They were all wonderful about the fact that we had no presents to open, but it still broke my heart. On top of that, Sierra told me stories. She said that, one time, Sue had thrown water in her face and then made her clean it up. Another time, when the family had been planning to go out to eat, Sierra had yelled at her sister, so Sue gave her a peanut butter sandwich at home and then only allowed Sierra a glass of water at the restaurant. And the worst of it was that Jay had been there both times.

How could he allow this to go on? I couldn't understand. All I could do was hope and pray that the Jay Ragina had once married would show up again and get a grip on matters—before the children had to suffer anymore. But when it seemed as if all of the bad were outweighing the good, it was hard to hope. I could only look for that day when God said enough was enough and set us all free.

By the end of the kids' stay, I was not feeling well, so Ken and Nikki took them back to California. I admit I might have been making excuses because I couldn't stand to take those kids back to a place I knew was not loving.

Not long after that, any last hope I had of the old Jay showing up went out the window, and my nightmare came true: I found out Sue was going to adopt the kids. What a joke. She didn't want those children. She only wanted the money and complete control over it.

God, how long are you going to allow this to go on? How far will you let it go? I read in your Word about how you come to the rescue and help the helpless. Well, these children are helpless, and I see no help for them! Please show up and revenge the hell they are going through. You also said, "Suffer the little children to come unto me and forbid them not." Well, these children have suffered more than any child should ever have to suffer. You know how Ragina raised her children in the church, and now that she has died, you are going to allow the devil and his sister to raise her children? I just don't understand any of this. I just want to give up so much of the time. It seems like we are fighting a losing battle, and you are nowhere to be found. Where are you, God! I need you, and I can't feel or see you in any of this. I am at my wit's end. How much more can I take?

As always, when the kids got home, all hell broke loose. Once again, I wasn't allowed to talk to them. I had been trying to get in touch with them for two weeks. Jay and Sue would put me on this roller-coaster ride every time I saw them, and now I was getting tired of it. Sue would answer and tell me the kids were not there, and most of the time she would say, "They can't talk right now." There was always an excuse. I didn't know if it was because Sue wanted to act as if Ragina had never lived or what the problem was, but this time, the gloves were off; I couldn't take any more of their crap.

I finally resolved to call Jay and tell him enough was enough, and to my surprise, he answered the phone. But he was like ice. I tried to break the ice with some small talk, but I was getting nowhere. Finally, I thought, *This is stupid. I might as well get to it and find out the problem.*

"Okay, Jay," I started in. "What in the hell have I done this time?" I asked, though I knew I had done nothing.

He started in with some bull about how Sierra had come home wanting to go back to Grandma's—and apparently, that was supposed to be my fault. Oh, and by the way, it was still sticking in his craw that I'd had a private investigator go to his mom's house the time Sierra was missing.

I said, "Wait a minute, Jay. We settled that. And I've had the kids twice since then."

"Well, it's things we're hearing from here in California too," he said.

"What in the hell are you hearing from California?"

"Just *stuff.*"

What a crock of crap this was. He wouldn't even tell me what he was hearing, let alone who he was hearing it from.

Finally, I pinned him down and he blamed it all on Sherry. She was Ragina's best friend. They had gone to school together and were like sisters, so I knew better than that. I laid it all out for him.

"Look, there are a few things sticking in my craw too. I don't really agree with some of the things you're allowing to happen to those kids. But I don't take it out on you, because my grandchildren are more important than what I think about things. But since you're going to go there, here's the deal. It gets pretty old when I have to hear all the things I hear, like Sierra being put in a garage and only given a peanut butter sandwich for dinner. Like Sue throwing water in Sierra's face and then making her clean it up. Like Sue pinning Sierra to the bed and screaming at her that she is bad and that bad little girls get sent away. Like Sue forcing Sierra to sleep on the bathroom floor. And like Sue checking out Renee's husband Tom before she checked you out, and then deciding that you had more to offer."

I stopped. There was only silence, so I continued. "I have kept all of this to myself until now, just to keep the peace ... but I see now that there is no keeping the peace. No matter what I do, you and Sue will make something of it." Jay was very mature about this; he just hung up on me. What a man.

Something had to give. I knew that Ragina had prayed a lot of prayers for her children and that those prayers would not go unanswered. But how much more could the devil do before God showed up and showed him he was on our side? How much longer before God unveiled all that was being done in secret and brought it to light? I knew it would happen; I just wished I knew when. I loved Jay, but I couldn't take anymore of this roller-coaster ride. It had to stop for Sierra. She did not deserve what was happening to her.

In the spring, Jay called and out of the blue, told me that he was not Sierra's real dad. He'd had a DNA test just to find out. I went to pieces. When I asked him why he'd even wanted the DNA test, all he would say is, "Because Ann is taller than Sierra." What a reason to have a DNA test. I was sure Ragina had told him. He'd known it from the beginning of their relationship together, but it hadn't made any difference until Sue entered the picture and apparently wanted Sierra out of it.

Not long after that, I called to talk to the children. I talked to Ann first, and then I asked to talk to Sierra.

"Sierra's not here, Grandma," Ann said.

"Where is she?"

"In her program."

"Okay, baby. Let me talk to your dad then."

There was a pause.

"Dad doesn't want to talk right now."

So I talked to Dakota instead. Then I hung up the phone and called Jay's cell.

"Hello?"

I couldn't believe he answered. "Where's Sierra?" I dove in.

"I put her in an RTC program," he said coldly. This was Lori's way of getting rid of Sierra.

"How long will she be there?"

"As long as it takes."

"Look, if you guys don't want Sierra, why don't you just let me come and get her?" I begged.

"There you go putting Sierra on a pinnacle again. As if she's special."

"Jay, she is very special"

"It's just a shame that you can't love the other two."

"You are crazy. I do love the other two—as much as I love Sierra. But you and Sue are not abusing the other two."

"You just don't understand," he said.

"You're right. I sure don't understand. I don't understand how someone can raise a child all his life and then turn on her. I can't understand why you'd even have a DNA test in the first place. And don't tell me again that it's because Ann is taller than Sierra."

It was at this point that I lost all faith that Jay would come around. He was such a disappointment. Here, all along, I had thought that he was such a good guy, and come to find out, he was a devil in the flesh. What Ragina had gone through with this man must have been unspeakable, and what he was now doing to Sierra was a crime. But no one was doing anything about it.

* * *

Sierra had been gone for about eight months, and Jay still would not tell me where she was, except for "in an RTC program." All I knew was that Sierra had told her teachers and school counslers befor she came up missing about what Sue and Jay had done to her at home, but then Jay and Sue would tell them that Sierra told lies. No one was listening to the child, but I was. And I was in the process of trying to find a lawyer who was willing to listen to me and to locate this innocent little girl. I knew God would get me to the right people so we could get Sierra out of this horrible place and give her the life she deserved. Jay and Sue had moved to New Mexico when things started to come to a head in California. People were beginning to take notice, but still no one had stepped up to help Sierra. I don't understand, but I guess our kids are not as safe as we think they are. Or if you have money and live in the newer part of town, no one investigates when a child tells them what is going on at home. So Jay and Sue were able to move to another state, and the abuse just kept getting worse.

I finally found an attorney in New Mexico. It was a miracle that he took my case. God must have touched his heart when I talked to him, because I didn't have a dime. And not only did he take me on; he also had a friend who was reportedly the best family attorney in New Mexico—an attorney named David Standridge. He was willing to take on the case and help us find Sierra.

Go figure, I thought. David was a man after God's own heart. It was no accident that these were the lawyers to help me. God was on the move.

Meanwhile, Jay had challenged me to find Sierra's real dad, and I knew he thought I could never do it, but guess what? A DNA test proved that a man name Tim Hagan was Sierra's dad. So now Jay and Sue didn't have a leg to stand on. Tim turned out to be a wonderful man with a loving, supportive wife. They had children together of their own. As soon as he heard my story about Sierra, he jumped on board, trying to help me and the attorneys find Sierra and get her out of Jay and Lori's care. Of course, Jay knew all along Sierra was not his biological child, but before Sue, it didn't matter. Why was he playing this DNA thing? He already knew. I guess it was to make Ragina look bad, like she kept the fact from him that Sierra was not his. I have stopped trying to understand it all.

To pay for the attorney's fees, Ken and I sold our two travel trailers and all of my diamond jewelry I had planned to hand down to my grandchildren. I was sad to see it go, but I knew it was worth it when I finally heard a court date announced: September 24, 2006.

On that day, I saw God's favor. We found out that Jay had put Sierra into a mental hospital in Albuquerque, New Mexico. I thought I would die when I heard that. There was nothing mentally wrong with Sierra. They'd only sent her there to get rid of her. But now that it was all coming out in the wash, I knew they would never be able to hurt her again.

We did not get Sierra back that day, but only because the judge was not comfortable taking anyone out of a mental hospital without first seeing the medical records.

While in court, we also sued for my grandparents' rights to see Ann and Dakota. I knew God would not allow these children to be taken away from the family, not to mention from the faith that their mother raised them in. So I was not too surprised when the judge granted me the right to see them, although I was elated. Jay was not. When the judge announced the court's decision, I thought Jay was having a high blood pressure attack, he turned so red.

It just went to show that if you do the right thing, everything will out in your favor. After all, I had done everything by the book and with much prayer, and now God was on our side. I knew there would still be a long way to go, however. Even though I now had the legal right to see the grandchildren, I knew Jay and Sue would continue to do everything in their power to give me grief over seeing them. But I was willing to keep fighting, because these children were Ragina's, and they were precious to me.

I asked to see Ann and Dakota while I was there. This was just five minutes after the judge had given me rights. I wanted to see them on this trip because they had been kept from me, and the judge asked how long I wanted to see them. My attorney told him, on my behalf, that I'd like to see them for about two to three hours, because I lived all the way in Oklahoma and had to leave the next morning.

"My client objects," said Jay and Lori's lawyer.

The judge looked at him. "And how long does your client want her to spend?"

After conferring with them, the lawyer responded, "Ten to fifteen minutes."

The judge looked up from his bench in disbelief. "What? What is the reason?"

Again the lawyer conferred with Jay and Lori, and then addressed the judge. "My clients are afraid she will run away with the children." This would have been funny if it weren't so sad to think people would show their ignorance in front of a court.

My attorney, David, jumped in. "Running away with the children would not work in my client's favor, since she is here to get custody of Sierra."

With that, the judge pointed at David, and said, "Done. Two hours tonight, from six thirty to eight thirty." Then he said I could see them as long as I gave a two-week notice. Needless to say, that was the last time I have seen them. Jay and Sue are in contempt of court. Every time I have called, they were going to be out of town or the kids had something going on that week.

I was so grateful, all I could do was cry.

Jay and Lori's attorney jumped in with a final request: his clients wanted my visit to be supervised. The judge granted this request, which was fine with me. The chaperone for the visit did not have to be government-appointed but could just be a mutual acquaintance. Besides, I had nothing to hide, and at least I still got to see my grandkids.

The plan that ensued was for Jay's sister Brenda (not her real name) to be the supervisor. She was to bring the children to the mall to meet us. When she arrived, however, there was another woman with her. Ken and Nikki and I had been sitting and waiting for them when the anonymous woman walked up to us, pointed at Nikki, and said, "She can't be here."

"Who are you?" I asked.

"A friend of the family's," she said.

"Well, you are not supposed to be here either," I said.

Apparently she didn't hear me or didn't understand, because she kept going. "She has to leave, or we will all leave and take the kids with us."

"If you do," I said, "I'll call the police. I have a court order stating the conditions of the visit, and you are not listed in it."

Then Nikki began to cry. "No, Grandma, you visit with the kids. I will go to the car."

At that point, Dakota and Ann also started to cry. All of their hearts were broken over this horrendous ordeal.

The other woman called Jay and Lori and told them that Nikki was there, and they continued to say that Nikki had to leave or else the two women were to leave and take the kids with them. So Nikki went to the car, and Ken went with her. Then we took turns being with the kids. Then I realized they didn't own the mall, so Nikki came into the food court. But when Ann and Dakota saw her, they ran to her. This must have touched the heart of the woman because she let them stay and Nikki too.

* * *

And as soon as the court was able to review Sierra's records from the mental hospital, they gave us permission to remove her. Sierra was able to leave and go live with her real dad, Tim, his wonderful wife, Jeri, and their beautiful kids.

To this day, I believe with all my heart that Sierra is in the place she is supposed to be. With Tim and Jeri, she has a wonderful life. She has two parents, two brothers, and a sister who really love her. I am so happy Tim is Sierra's dad because they are a wonderful family. Sierra and her dad go hunting together. They are a very outdoorsy family and do everything together: hunting, fishing, horseback riding, and camping. Sierra lives in Colorado and has become a real little cowgirl.

Jeri and Tim invited me to come to Colorado to see Sierra anytime. I flew up there to visit, but before going, I asked Tim, "Where is the nearest hotel to your house?"

He replied, "The nearest hotel is our house. You are welcome to stay here, and we would be insulted if you didn't."

I had made the plans to go. I wasn't sure how Jeri would feel. After all, I was Ragina's mom. I had met her at New Mexico at court when she came with Tim so we could find and get Sierra, and she was wonderful. But as soon as I got there, I felt as if I was at one of my own children's house. I was received with so much love. Jeri, Sierra, and I sat at the table and talked. For the first time since the accident, Sierra was allowed to talk about her mom, and Jeri sat there and cried with us. I can't explain the wonderful heart this woman has and how lucky Sierra is to have Jeri in her life. Sierra now calls Jeri Mom, and if anyone has earned that title, Jeri has. For all the hell Jay and Sue put her through, she is going to be a wonderful lady, and I always said they could not break her because she had her mother's will.

I have wondered many times who hears the cry of the innocent. The things I had found out that were happening to Sierra were horrifying. Even her teachers had seen some of it and never came to her rescue. She had been made to sleep in the bathroom floor. On Christmas Day, when my niece went to give the children their Christmas presents, she asked where Sierra was and was told by Jay and Sue she was being punished and was locked in the bathroom. I found out from one of Jay and Ragina's best friends—I'll call him Robert (not his real name)—that he was at Jay's after the death of Ragina, and Jay and Sue had other people over. Jay stripped Sierra down to her underwear and hosed her down with a water hose in front of his friends. Jay and all his friends were drunk, so they had a good laugh. But Robert was horrified because he had also been a good friend to Ragina and knew how much her children meant to her, so he left. That's it—he just left. Who hears the cry of the innocent? Not many. It is sad when friends and teachers know things are not right but do nothing.

Richard

[M]y son was dead, and is alive again;
he was lost, and is found.
—Luke 15:24

Out of the blue, one day, Richard, Renee's next-to-the-oldest son and only remaining child in California, called me. He sounded troubled.

"Grandma, I really need help," he said. "Before I end up in jail or hurting myself or someone else."

He was by now legally considered of age and had had no help from anyone since the accident, even though he had been ejected from the car and thrown to the pavement so hard that he'd gotten a thousand stitches in his back. He'd chosen to stay with his stepfather, even though the rest of his siblings were with me now, and even though Tom was going through so much grief himself that he was no emotional help to Richard. The result? Richard turned to drugs so he could just be "out of it" most of the time and forget about everything that was happening. Thank God it was only for a time, however. Eventually, he got himself out of it.

"Grandma, I just got tired of the drugs," he told me after admitting to smoking pot and drinking. Then he told me a horror story about how he once slept on a bench at K-Mart. It broke my heart.

The good thing was that he admitted it; I didn't have to coax it out of him. I feel the reason that half the battle is to admit you need help is because God can only do something with someone who will admit his needs. And this child really wanted help.

I told him that I had been praying for him and that I wanted him to come live with us so he could have a second chance in life. And so it was that Richard arrived on Sunday, June 30. He seemed like he was already feeling better by the time he got here, but it was clear he still needed a lot of help. When I saw him on our doorstep, I just knew that God had sent him here so he could get the help he needed. But that, too, would not be without its challenges.

I was soon to find out that Richard's anger got out of hand quickly, even though after his outbursts, he was always so sorry. But sorry wouldn't help if he was hurting or had hurt someone else. I took him to a psychologist that John Burnett, one of the lawyers in Sierra's case, told us about.

I was so pleased when the psychologist met us with a, "Praise God. You made it!" He was a Christian man. I wasn't sure how Richard would take it, but he seemed to really liked Dr. Godsent. (That's not his real name, but he was God sent.) I liked that, before we left each session, the doctor asked to pray with us. Once again, God had sent someone to our rescue. And once again, God had gotten us to the right place at the right time. That was just like God—to surprise you when you least expected it by having one of his people in place to help in your time of need.

Richard went through a lot of anger issues even after counseling. He went back to California and then came back again. This was about the time we moved to El Reno, Oklahoma. Richard was doing well, but wouldn't you know it, the devil raised his evil head in another attempt to destroy Richard and me. I knew something was wrong. Richard was not acting right, and the anger was getting really bad again.

Then one day he just went off. I was afraid Ken might hurt Richard if he started to put holes in the walls of our home. He had done that in every house we had ever lived in, so I told Ken to go on I could handle it, not knowing it was not going to work this time. We were in the living room and I was screaming and begging Richard to calm down. By the way, screaming is not the way to calm someone down, but that's what I did. Before I knew it, Richard had attacked me, and I was them screaming for help. That's the time to scream.

We ended up on the floor, and I looked into his eyes. I knew my Richard was no longer there and the drugs had taken over. I thought, *My God what am I to do?* I knew he was going to kill me. If he knew what he was doing, I was never afraid of him, but now I was dealing with the influence drugs had on him. I asked God to help me, and he did, because the next thing I knew, this grandma came with a left hook that sent him across the room. Still not knowing what to do, I got up, ran to my bedroom, and shut my door. There was Ken's gun. I would never shoot one of my grandchildren, even if they were going to kill me; okay, maybe in the foot to stop them from attacking me.

I can write this now because God has worked it all out. Richard did go back to California, but I was out there a few months ago. We had a wonderful time. We went out to dinner, and he is doing great. So anyone has come too late to tell me that we had family problems and haven't talked for years. What a crock. Forgiveness is a choice, and I choose to live a life of love and forgiveness. God is love, and if you can't love and forgive, you don't have God.

Nikki

The LORD his God ...
executeth judgment for the oppressed.
—Psalm 146:5, 7

Nikki was out of control. She was starting to be verbally abusive and had attacked both Ken and me. Probably the worst of these attacks happened during one of the times when Sierra was staying with us. I had told Danni she could take Sierra to the dollar store in Nikki's car, and Nikki pushed me from behind. I turned around and held her arms to restrain her, and she ended up taking a hunk out of my arm with her car keys.

And then I had one more thing to face: I began having severe back pain. I was down for about two months before I finally gave in and decided to spend the money to have a doctor look at it. After having some tests done, it turned out I had three ruptured discs in my back, and the only way to fix them was to have surgery—rods, pins, fusions, the whole works. What did I do now? I supposed just the same thing I had always done. I trusted God to see me through and get me back on my feet. It wasn't a matter of being strong; it was a matter of knowing where my only help came from. My strength came from the Lord, so I would trust in him.

The surgery was not to be, however. After another test came in, and it turned out that I had osteoporosis so bad that there was nothing to which they could connect the hardware that they'd have had to put in my back. I said I would take my healing any way God wanted to give it; I had thought it was going to be surgery, but now I was waiting for my miracle. It would come.

I returned from the hospital just in time to deal with more of Nikki's drama. She asked to go tan at 10:30 at night, and when I said no, she exploded.

"You will let me go, or I will leave!" she screamed. "You are only saying no because you're in pain!"

To me, she was being very disrespectful. But I was in pain, so I said, "Fine, go."

And go she did—but not to tan. Instead, she left and moved in with her boyfriend's family. I blamed myself. I had been in such a state of depression from the death of my daughters and being down with back pain that I had let her get out of hand. The first time I told her no about something, she left. She had met this boy at church. Go figure that one. At first I was really happy that maybe she had found a good guy who would treat her right.

When she told me she was going to move in with her boyfriend's family, what I should have done was to tell her to get back in her room and stay there until she turned of age. But instead I said, "Go if's that's what you want." True, I was in no shape to deal with her drama, but that was not an excuse for me not doing what was right.

The next day, I tried to call her several times, but she would only reply with texts. I was hoping she was taking a second look at what she had done, but then again, I knew her. She wanted to have her cake and eat it too. I thought just maybe being with this other family for a while would teach her that no family was perfect—that there were problems in everyone's life. But there was nothing I could say to her to change her mind. I knew at this point I had spoiled her so much that she had lost all respect for me and didn't care what I said. And she likely didn't even care what she said to me or how badly it hurt.

A couple of weeks later, Nikki came over and started talking about coming home. I told her that I felt to blame because I had spoiled her so badly that she had come to think this would be acceptable behavior. Then I told her that we loved her and that she always had a home here. She seemed to be softening up to me until she asked me if I could do something for her. When I told her I couldn't do it right then but could do it a couple of days later, she stormed out.

After that, we filed for a pickup order to have Nikki brought home. This was because she was considered a runaway. In response, I got a letter in the mail from an attorney. When I opened it, I almost had another stroke. Nikki and her boyfriend's mother and sister had gone to court and gotten an emergency custody order putting them in charge of Nikki. It was a temporary order. We were to go court on March 28 to dispute it, but this was still a nightmare. This one was really in God's hands.

When I got that letter, I felt like I did at the time of the accident—numb and in shock. I just couldn't bring myself to believe it. This was total betrayal by the granddaughter to whom we'd given everything. Such a betrayal was surely the second-worst thing that could happen to a family, the first being the loss of its children—and now both had happened to us. It felt as though we had experienced another death in the family.

As I thought about how I should have handled Nikki differently from the very beginning, I found myself crying and having panic attacks. I knew she had wanted to be with her boyfriend, but I never thought she would go this far. And how could the boy's mother just sit there and let it all happen without even talking to me about things first? The only reason Nikki had done all this was so she could move in with her boyfriend—and his mother and sister were just okay with that? There had to be something else. And I had a feeling that the plot was just starting to thicken.

Again, God came to the rescue. He sent me Psalm 146, in which he said he would execute justice for the oppressed and heal the brokenhearted. What did I do from here? I didn't know. All I knew was that if I left it in God's hands, it would all work out.

After a few days of running it over and over in my mind, it dawned on me: the attorney's letter and paperwork had said they'd filed for custody of Nikki "and her estate." That mom knew about the wrongful-death lawsuit we had against Ford Motor Company and Cooper Tires. This was filed because upon investigating the cause of the accident, they found that the tire on Ragina's car were defective and that the car itself was not safe.

She knew that Nikki stood to get a large sum of money from it, and as long as they had custody of her, they had custody of her estate. Man did it all make sense to me now. They were taking advantage of a little girl who thought she was in love but who was actually just the victim of post-traumatic stress disorder and raging hormones.

I told myself that as soon I found out how far this had gone and who all was involved, there might be someone doing jail time. How outsiders could step in and help a child destroy a family that had already lost everything, I couldn't understand for the life of me.

Don't get me wrong. I was in no way trying to put all of the blame on this boy's family. I knew Nikki. I had covered for her many times, not letting people know the real truth. Not telling them about her verbal abuse and physical attacks. Not showing them the deep scar on my arm from her car keys. There are things she did that I am not, even now, comfortable putting in this book. But this latest trick was the last straw because she had involved other people—and the wrong kind of people. They were people, who, unbeknownst to her, were trying to take her for all she was worth. My only hope was that if the law didn't save this child, God would.

I don't know what I would have done during this time had it not been for Joann and Jerry Lebouef. Joann and I had been friends for twenty years, and she was a sister in every way but by blood, although sometimes we wondered about that too. If not for Joann and Jerry, we would not have had food this month since Nikki, by direction of you-know-who, went to the Social Security office and got her $856 for that month. This was Ken's Social Security. The office turned it over to her because after the adoption, the girls were able to draw on Ken's Social Security. God had always sent Joann to the rescue. She was such a blessing in my life and ministry. She had such a humble heart and a wonderful ministry of helping others and was an armor-bearer for me in my own ministry. I had watched her grow in God over the years, and I knew God had put us together for such a time as this.

God eventually worked things out for us and Nikki as well. At my request, she came home one day to meet with an advisor from her school. Nikki was now in her senior year and had seemed to lose all ability to concentrate in class. Plus, her grades were slipping so dramatically that we were going to have to remove her, and I could not get Nikki to talk about any of it. This was particularly troubling because Nikki had been an honor roll student for the first three years of high school. She'd had her head on straight, had set some pretty high goals for herself, and had been working hard to reach them. The advisor recommended that Nikki move back home to help her cope with some of the stress she was going through and get things back in order so that she could graduate.

Later, Nikki confided to me that all she could think about was that she was going to graduate and that her mom would not be here to see her. We both cried. And after talking to a doctor and to her school principal, we all agreed that in order for her to graduate, her being homebound was the answer. But Nikki didn't come home at that time. Her boyfriend's dad checked her out of school and put her in a school in another town. He could do this because they had the temporary custody order.

Looking back, I believe the whole situation occurred as a result of Nikki going through a depression, although it didn't help that she also hated the way her grandpa cussed and ranted around the house. I explained to her that it was just his way of dealing, although I agreed that I sure wished he would find a different outlet.

"But one thing I have learned," I told her, "is that you can't control how people deal with loss." It was true. In fact, I had come to believe that this was a major factor in many people divorcing after a family crisis—everyone was trying to control how everyone else handled the crisis, and it just caused more trauma.

And it was the same now for Nikki. "We love and miss you very much," I told her. "And I am glad you're coming back home. But you must work this out for yourself." It was just our job to love her, and to be there for her when she needed it most.

After much heartbreak and trauma, I'm happy to say Nikki is doing wonderful has a beautiful baby girl. I am very proud of her.

John and Danielle
— and Dannielle

And the woman conceived, and bare a son
—Exodus 2:2

John and Danielle became pregnant. Both of them were so young, and of course, neither had a mom to help, so it was all up to me. They were two young, married babies having a baby. I started by helping Dani find a doctor. I wanted to do the very best for them and give them the guidance they so needed. They were such good kids and had a hard road to travel with only their grandfather and me to help them. Several months later, they had a healthy baby, and things were going well. They had a little girl. She looked just like her mom—so beautiful. And Danielle was such a wonderful mother. She took such good care of the baby and never seemed to let the late nights or sleepless night get to her. I was so proud of her and John, being so young yet taking on so much adult responsibility.

But then, when their beautiful little girl was four, they had another baby girl. They had moved to California. I was going out for the new baby, and then out of the blue, I received a dreaded call. The baby had suddenly died. Danielle was nine months along, and the baby was healthy, or so we all thought. My God, what had happened now? It had only been five years since John had lost his mom and sister, not to mention his aunt, who was a second mom to him. My heart was broken, though I knew I could do nothing. But I did let him know that I was there if he needed me. After all, I knew what it was to lose a child. I had lost every child I'd ever had. I went for the baby's funeral. John and

63

Danielle were devastated. No one seemed to know why the baby had died so suddenly. The autopsy had not come back, but the results were the same; we had lost yet another one

Dannielle also became pregnant. She was only sixteen. I did not even know she was dating. I knew all the kids went out as a group, but little did I know it was just a front for Dannielle to be with James (not his real name). Right after she broke the news, I thought, *I can't take this!* We got through it just fine, though, and she had a wonderful, blue-eyed boy who I would not trade for anything in the world.

Ken and I took him in, and now Cameron is in his terrible twos. I never dreamed I would be raising teenagers at my age, much less a baby. Danni told me that people were giving her a hard time because her grandfather and I were raising Cameron, but I told her it took more love to do what was best for your child than to allow him to be in a situation that may not be in his best interest just because of what others were saying.

I was so angry, though, because I was getting the same kinds of comments. People would say thing, like, "If I were you, I'd make her take her son." But the point is they were not me, and they had no idea of what was going on. But those were usually people who didn't have a clue as to what our family had been through. But until you walk in someone's shoes, you don't really know what you would do. It's easy to give advice when you are on the outside looking in. And I know people were just trying to help me and most of the time were worried about what I was going through. I thank God that I was loved that much.

Besides, Cameron was such a blessing to Ken and me. He brought a joy into a home full of pain—a joy that we thought we would never have again. He was a constant reminder that, so many times, what the enemy meant to do to destroy, God could turn into a blessing. And that is exactly what happened with Cameron.

That didn't mean that I would try to keep Cameron from Danni, however. She loved him with all her heart, and as soon as she was ready to take him, I would let him go.

Danni eventually ended up back home. Of course, I had half expected it. I'd known all along that her boyfriend had not been good for her, but she had to find that out for herself. I had gone through hearing a lot of advice from a lot of people, telling me how to handle the situation, but again, I knew that if I put her situation in God's hands, it would all turn out okay.

Cameron is now five years old and still with NaNa and PaPa. Dannielle is married and has a beautiful one-year-old baby girl named Addysan who also loves her nana and papa. We went through a lot. Dannielle had post-partum depression after Addysan was born and could not even hold her, but now Addysan is a mama's girl and loves being with her mom. Dannielle is on the road to recovery from drugs and alcohol. It has been a long, hard road, but God never left us.

Ken

I have heard thy prayer, I have seen thy tears:
behold, I will add unto thy days.
—Isaiah 38:5

This whole time, it seemed that all hell was breaking loose in Ken. He was out of control. He went off on a rampage nearly every day, yelling and cursing. Half the time, I swore he was losing it, but I didn't know what to do except put it in God's hands and let his anger run its course. I figured it was his way of dealing with the grief, the stress, and the financial strain we were under.

We were in one fight for a week straight, and it escalated every day. I'm not even sure how or if we resolved it, but I had grown so tired of the fighting. All it achieved was to heap more stress on top of what was already there. At times, it seemed unbearable, and I felt as if I were going to go crazy.

And then one day, I got a call—one of those phone calls you don't want to get. The man on the other end was Ken's buddy William. Ken and William had gone out with two other guys, Billy and Tommy, to put up deer stands in the woods. They were getting ready for hunting season.

"Sister Thelma, everything is all right," was the first thing William said, which told me that everything was not all right.

"What happened?" I asked.

"They have Ken and Tommy in the hospital. A deer stand fell on Ken."

I had seen deer stands. They were these steel ladder-looking contraptions that you stood up against a tree. Right? Wrong. This was a stand that had been made out of steel as well as out of two-by-sixes and two-by-fours—and we're not just talking about a few sheets of lumber but seven hundred pounds' worth.

Ken's hip was out of place, and he needed surgery as soon as possible. He had only a five-hour window to get it repaired, or he ran the risk of being permanently crippled. I called and lined up the best hip surgeon in the country, a doctor in Fort Smith, Arkansas. The surgeon told me to have Ken airlifted to the hospital, since there was a time crunch, and then promised that he would be there waiting for Ken upon his arrival.

I relayed the message, telling the local hospital to airlift him to Fort Smith. So what did they do? That's right. They put him in an ambulance for a two-and-a-half-hour ride. If he'd have been airlifted, he would have had about three hours to spare. But as it was, he was two or three hours past the five-hour window, so we had to wait to see whether Ken was going to need a complete hip replacement or if he would be okay.

If I couldn't have seen so clearly what the devil was up to, I would've crawled right back into my tunnel. But I knew this was spiritual warfare. And I knew who won spiritual warfare—those who allowed God to do the fighting. This battle was not mine but the Lord's. In that moment, I felt like Job when he said, "Though God slay me, yet I'll trust him." God was the one who created me, and in turn, he was the only one who could take care of me. It wasn't always in the way I would choose, but it was always in the way he saw fit, and God always knew best.

As it was, we were just lucky Ken was alive. After hearing the whole story from the guys, I was sure that this, in itself, was a miracle from God. The other three men said the deer stand had fallen right on top of Ken; he had been right under it. And then, all of a sudden, they said, the stand flew off of him. Not only that, but it landed about fifteen feet away. Now I don't know much about deer stands, but I know that seven hundred pounds of wood and steel is not just going to bounce; it's going to stay where it falls. Except for when an angel gets under it. And an angel could throw such a structure fifteen feet away. Don't believe in angels? Then you tell me how it got off of him.

At first, the other men thought Ken was dead. He had blood coming out his mouth and nose and had been totally crushed. But then he looked up at William before his eyes closed and his head fell over. At that point, every man fell to their knees and began to call out to God. Ken then not only came to but also was able to speak.

"I'm hurt bad," he said to Billy. "You hunt my deer stand this year." That sounds just like him.

Billy began to scream, "No, no I won't!" Then he called out to William, "Call nine-one-one. He's alive!"

When Ken returned home from the hospital, he was laid up for awhile, forcing us to live on disability income. But I was just thankful for what a wonderful God we have. He had been right there and had heard the prayers of those three men, calling out in the woods for the life of their friend. Ken ended up having to have a full hip replacement, but it did crush some of the ranting out of him. I don't know if he didn't fell like ranting and raving or just realized it didn't change things, but he had calmed down—for now at least.

Part IV

Finding My Way Out

The Light at the End

And they called the blind man, saying unto him,
Be of good comfort, rise; he calleth thee.
And he, casting away his garment, rose, and came to Jesus.
—Mark 10:49–50

I don't know exactly when it happened, except for that it was after one of my trips to California. I had gone there to yet for another family disaster. I was feeling as if all I would ever do was wait for the next shoe to fall. While I was there, I had visited with my nephew, Pastor Ron. He had told me I would not come back from California the same, and he was right, although I didn't know it at first.

As soon as I returned home, I was looking for some great revelation of God—some epiphany. I was waiting for some momentous occasion at church or at a prayer meeting that resulted in dancing and shouts of praise. But nothing like that happened. Then one day, I woke up—and suddenly felt as if I were really *here*. That's when it dawned on me that this was the "different" the pastor had been talking about. After all, that's usually how God works, isn't it? Not through dancing and shouting, not through an earthquake or a fire but through a still, small voice (1 Kings 19:12). I knew in my heart that God could take the most hopeless situation and turn it into an outright victory, but I would have to let God do it for me because I could not see any victory in myself.

In the hours and days that followed, it was as if my eyes were now opened, allowing me to see not only everything that had been lost through these horrible experiences but also all of the many, many things that had been gained. I could see that, although I had lost my two daughters and my granddaughter all at the same time, they had gained heaven—and what was more, they had been able to do it together. My girls had always been together in life, and they had stayed together through death. And thinking about it in that way somehow helped me feel glad they were in that car together and that neither one had to die alone.

I had always known that my girls were in heaven, but now I felt it too and actually began to feel grateful for it. I could now thank God that they were safe with him for eternity and that I wouldn't ever have to worry about them again, either for their safety or for what Satan might drag them into. And I remembered that my children were not only in my past but in my future as well. I reveled in the idea that I would be with them again and that we would spend eternity together in heaven.

Of course, I still grieved for them every day and missed them more than words could say, but what was different now was that I really had faith that they were okay and that we would be together again. I thanked God for that faith, because it's what gave me the assurance of knowing that this was not the end of my children but only the beginning for them in a place where they would never have to face sadness, pain, or temptation again. What did parents do who didn't have that hope? How did they make it through the day? I knew the hope that I'd had in God, and still, I had been in the tunnel for more than seven years.

Another difference: I could see too that, although I had the added stress and expenses of caring for my grandchildren, I also had a wonderful, large new family full of people who loved me and had been so good to me through the years. How blessed I had been to have them.

My eyes were also opened to two recent miracles. One was a new set of tires for my car, which allowed me to drive to California. The other was the money to go there, because by this time, we could not even pay our bills, much less go on a trip. I was riding on one miracle, and every time I put gas in my car was the other. All I could think was, *I can't wait to see what God is going to do.*

A third miracle had happened just when I had thought I was about to lose my mind over the situation with Sierra when Cowboy Tim and his wonderful wife Jeri came to my granddaughter's rescue. I knew that had been no accident. God had had that in hand from the very start.

How blind I had been. All this time, I hadn't been able to see what was right in front of me because I was looking either too far ahead or somewhere behind.

For seven-and-a-half years, I had just gone through the motions of living but was not really living. There was no telling what I had said to people because I had not actually been alive but was only breathing in and out, putting one foot in front of the other. I had died on the side of the road that night along with my daughters and granddaughter and had buried myself with them in the grave. The only difference between them and me was that I had been walking around for the past seven-plus years. They were who I was, and without them, I didn't know how to be me. After they died, I didn't know who I was anymore. They had been my life, and without them, I thought that I had no life and that there was nothing else worth living for.

In turn, I had only gone through the motions of raising my grandchildren but had not really been there, and now ... my God ... my home was in foreclosure, my car payment was two months behind, and I had only nine dollars left to buy milk and diapers for the week. After all, since Ken's surgery, his only earnings had come in the form of regular disability checks, making our income half of what it had been. Still, in some miraculous, unexplainable way, I was at peace.

Had I realized the dire situation we were in just three months before, I would have melted and had nervous breakdown. Now—though I didn't know why—I just no longer let my circumstances control my emotions. Maybe I got to a point where I realized that I couldn't change them anyway, so I had no choice but to give everything to God to take care of. I began, often, to pray my own version of the prayer of Jabez, found in 1 Chronicles 4:10: "Oh, that you would bless me indeed, and enlarge my territory, that your hand would be with me and that you would keep me from evil that I may not cause pain." This was his prayer when he called on the God of Israel, and that is the same God that I call on. And I know he hears my prayer.

My time of grieving was still not over, but my time of living had begun. I had once thought that I would never feel anything again, but praise God, now I felt the life coming back into me. I could say with conviction that I foresaw a time when I would be able to leave the darkness and return to the light. And I could see that I was finally beginning to exit the place of hopelessness in which I had lived for so very long.

I knew that by keeping my faith in God and doing my best to serve him, I would make it through to the other side, just like Job did, because

Jesus loved me and was not the one who had done this to our family. But Jesus was the one who would get us through.

In addition, I knew that if I didn't waver and give up, God would give me back double for my trouble. By this point, we had lost almost everything—the cabin, the two travel trailers, the car, and our health in some cases, and now it was about to be our house. But praise God that I had finally reached a place in which I could confidently serve warning on Satan, knowing that everything he had stolen from my family, he would return double, just as he'd had to with Job, because God would not let this debt go unpaid. My miracle was on the way, and when it got there, all the world would know that God never lets his children down and that his blessings are well worth the wait.

A minister friend of mine who lost his son in a car accident often told a story about how he had asked God never to take one of his children. After the accident, he had told God, "You did not live up to our agreement. You let my son die in that car." But then he realized that God had never promised anything. The pastor was the one who had made the deal; he had just assumed that God would go along with it. But what he found out was that, no matter what we face, we must realize that God is still God, and we are still human, which means we don't have the understanding that God has about every situation. So whatever happens in our lives, it is our place to keep the faith, while it is God's place to keep us in his care.

It had been a long, dark journey through that tunnel, but now I was finally seeing a light at the end. Now I wanted to do something to honor my daughters and my parents, but also, most of all, to honor the God of my life, who had brought me through. The alpha and the omega, the beginning and the end. Looking back, I knew that he had been with me all along, even when I doubted, because had he not been, I would have never made it this far. He had been with me since day one of that terrible accident, and I felt assured now that he would continue to guide me out of this deep, dark place.

Life on the Other Side

We are troubled on every side, yet not distressed; we are perplexed,
but not in despair;
Persecuted, but not forsaken; cast down, but not destroyed
—2 Corinthians 4:8–6329

*F*inally, at some undetermined time, I did emerge from the tunnel. I knew that I had reached the other side, because I could suddenly see the stars again when I looked into the sky. It had been so long that I'd forgotten how beautiful they were.

The things around me were coming to life again. I loved seeing the flowers bloom and the leaves on the trees. I could actually feel air enter my lungs. I was breathing, walking, and talking and not just going through the motions.

But there was a flipside to all of this feeling and seeing and breathing and living: because I had renewed expectations and hope in my life, I now took the bad days more to heart. When Nikki or Dannielle would act out, for example, I would suddenly feel devastated. For some reason, I expected that on this side of the tunnel the girls would respect me again. I think I even expected the pile of bills to magically dwindle. Worst of all, I expected just to feel better all of the time; to stop feeling the pain and the grief, and to just permanently be all right. But that was not the case.

Some days, in fact, I thought I liked being back in the tunnel better, since at least then I hadn't known night from day. In the tunnel, I could just breathe in and out, and not feel, and not be. In the darkness, nothing really mattered, and that was okay. But now that I had seen daylight, I knew that I had to be accountable for my actions again. I had to make responsible decisions. I had to cope. The problem was, I had been out of it so long that I felt I no longer knew how to do that.

The hardest time to do this was during holidays and anniversaries of the girls' death. Around those times, the feelings would all start coming back to me as if the accident had just happened, although the reason often didn't hit me until I was in the path of the tornado. I would be doing well and holding things together, and then, all of a sudden, I wanted to jump out of my skin and couldn't figure out why. It would hit so fast and hard, it was like a two-ton steel ball had knocked me over without warning. I would get that sick feeling in the pit of my stomach and the sensation that I couldn't breathe. And only then I would realize that it was because I was coming upon another anniversary or holiday.

Mother's Day was particularly hard. The first Mother's Day after the accident, I had wanted to run as fast and as far away as possible. You couldn't help but look at all the mothers and their children together in church or out to eat, and it only made your loss feel more real in that moment.

I continued to have a hard time on each anniversary of the accident, as well. Even until very recently, I didn't want to talk to anyone or go anywhere on those days. I just wanted to be alone, although that was the worst thing I could do, because being alone gave the devil an opportunity to torment my mind. Now I know that I have to get up and get out and do something—and the best thing I know how to do to help me through is to do something for the kingdom of God. It would help if I could touch one person or give someone else who was in a dark place hope or if I could take the focus off myself and use my life to help just one person with a word or a prayer.

On the six-year anniversary of the girls' deaths, I am proud to say, I was able to tell myself that just because it was hard didn't give me the right to throw in the towel, especially when so many people were depending on me. I was at Wal-Mart in Fort Smith, Arkansas, and saw a family who was there taking pictures with their son who was being deployed to war. I went to the girl who was taking the pictures and spoke to her out of earshot of anyone and asked her how much the pictures were. She told me, and I paid for them and left. I told her when they were through to tell them that I said thank you for the young man who was going to fight for our freedom and my prayers were for his safe return. I still pray for that young man today. I don't know his name, but God does. To give out of faith and expect nothing in return was such a wonderful feeling.When we open our hearts to give, it opens a path for God to return the blessing, and he does over and over again.

These occasions have taught me, more than ever, to depend on God. It's sometimes all I can do just to ask God to get me through it one more time. And he always has, so I know he always will. And no, depending on him is not always easy. But getting started is. You just say to yourself, "God is the only one who can keep me sane, so my only choices are to trust God or go insane." From there, the decision you make is a no-brainier. You trust God.

Consistently acting on that decision, however, is the hard part. Oh sure, anyone can cop out and stay hyped up on drugs and forget the world around him or her, but what kind of life is that? If you find yourself falling into that trap of going back into the darkness, it can help to ask yourself, "Is that what my late loved ones would want me to do? Or would they want me to step up, allow God to heal my pain, and stay the person they knew, respected, and loved?" Especially when grandchildren are involved, it's time to think of something besides ourselves.

Again, that isn't always easy. But through God, it can be done. I couldn't say this unless I had lived it, and I have. I will continue to live it until Jesus comes. There is no bringing my children back, so I must live to go to them. I fight every day just to keep myself going, but I know it is what my girls would have wanted. I want to honor them by not letting all this destroy me.

The other challenge I faced on the other side of the tunnel was dealing with criticism and self-doubt. Sometimes I felt like people were saying about me what they said about Paul in Acts 27. Paul had just survived a storm and a shipwreck when a viper attached itself to him. The people who saw it happen were saying, "He must be a murderer or have done something else wrong, because the gods are not letting him escape." Paul just shook the snake off into the fire and went about his business. Suddenly, those same people thought Paul must be a god.

When I got out of the tunnel, it seemed to me that people nowadays were just as fickle. When all hell was being turned loose on you, they assumed it must be your fault; but as soon as you won the victory, you were an okay person again. I knew that there were people asking themselves, and maybe even others, "What did Thelma do that caused all of this to happen to her?" I often felt like approaching these people and saying, "Well, join the crowd, because I ask myself the same question all the time!" I would have been the first to admit that some of my "snakes" had been the result of wrong choices. But undeniably, there were also those times when Satan was just trying to stir up my life and make me doubt in God—and it was in those instances that I had to learn to shake off the snake, shake off the criticism, and just trust God, because bad things happen to good people just as sure as good things happen to bad people.

On the flip side, other people said to me, "I wish I had your faith" or "I wish I could be as strong as you." The first thing I wanted to say was, "You don't know the road I have had to travel. But if you want to be like me, I can pray for you to lose all your children and have to raise your grieving grandchildren while you just try to make it from one day to the next." Of course, I never did say that and I never would, but the point is that people were still judging me by my outward appearance and behavior when they didn't really know what I faced to be in the place I was in. They were trying to mimic me rather than to be the best they could be in the lives God had granted them and trying to find his will for *their* lives.

Even as recently as a year ago, if I would mention feeling pain over the loss of my girls, some people would look at me like, "It's been seven years. It's time to let it go!" But of course, these people's children were all still alive and well.

What I learned from all of this in the end was that just as people are prone to judge you by what is happening in your life or how you handle it outwardly, God is also looking at how you deal with it in your heart. As for me, I didn't always handle things well, or even in the right way, but through it all, I figured out that the most important thing was to keep my eyes on Jesus and not on the others watching me. Like Paul, I'd shake my snake off into the fire and move on, trusting God.

At times, it was very tempting to crawl back into that dark place and stay there. It would have been easier to go numb and check out of reality again than to feel pain and to be accountable for what was going on around me. But it also would've been more cowardly. In fact, after coming out of the other side of the tunnel and looking back, there were times when I wondered whether I had honestly faced anything in my whole life. I could see how, even before the accident, I ran from the hard things in life by trying to forget about them and concentrate on other people's problems.

Now I could no longer run. I had no choice but to face things head-on. My children were gone. How could I run from that? I was living in the reality of it every day, so I had to learn to face it and let God help me through. I would never have gotten this far if it had not been for God, and I know he will not leave me now.

My entire lifestyle has to flow from faith. That is not always the easiest way to live, but it is the only way to live if I really want life. I must live life by faith. There are things that will happen to all of us that we don't like or agree with, so we all have to learn to let go and let God work out every situation. We can turn that thing around that Satan meant for our destruction and use it for victory.

When faced with tragedy, we all have a choice. We can use that tragedy to check out of life, or we can use it for the glory of God and not let the devil win. I am at a point in my life now where I want to use my tragedy to further the kingdom of God. I was in that tunnel for so long that I feel I have accomplished almost nothing to that end. It's time to get started. I want to use the life I've been given to help God's other children who are suffering from loss. I want to turn my suffering into hope for those in that long, dark tunnel who feel there is no way out.

That is why, in the next section of this book, I offer up the life lessons that I have learned from my harrowing journey. Although I know my grief is not over and that I have many more lessons to learn, my prayer is that those still in the darkness may use the ideas that follow to help them more quickly get through their own long, dark tunnels.

Part V

Offering Hope

Time to Grieve

To everything there is a season, and a time to every purpose under the heaven....
A time to weep, and a time to laugh; a time to mourn, and a time to dance.
—Ecclesiastes 3:1, 4

After the loss of a loved one, especially a child, be assured that there will be a time for healing, but healing does not happen overnight. In fact, sometimes healing does not happen over years. However long it may take you to get through that long, dark tunnel is okay, though, because grief is different for each of us. Allow yourself the time *you* need to grieve.

You may also feel or express your grief differently from others. That's fine too. The main thing is that you allow yourself to feel the loss, because only then can you get to a place of healing.

As different as the experience is for each of us, however, the process of grieving brings with it the same emotions for everyone—shock, denial, anger, guilt, and emptiness.

Shock and Denial

On the way to the hospital in Amarillo on the night of the accident, I kept thinking, *When we get there, my girls will be okay, and all the grandchildren will be okay. This happens to other families, not to us.*

Then, among the buzz that followed—hospital staff escorting us through the halls, the sight of Nikki and Sierra severely wounded, the news that both my children and my granddaughter were gone forever—nothing felt real. I was walking and talking, but I was not present. I kept thinking, *There has been an awful mistake. In a minute, someone is going to tell me they either made an error or played a very cruel joke. This is not happening to my children.*

This was shock and denial—the feeling that I was living in a dream and would wake up any second to find my girls alive and well. Deep down, I knew that was not true—that the reality was they were gone and my life would never be the same. But how could I accept that? If I admitted they weren't coming back, I would not be able to go on. I was sure the pain would kill me.

Anger and Abandonment

When I finally admitted that my loss was not only real but also permanent, I experienced terrible anger and emptiness. There were times I wanted to throw things and scream, and I learned that doing so was okay as long as I did not hurt anyone.

I would get angry at God for allowing such a traumatic thing to happen to me and my family. I would get angry at my daughters for abandoning me, and at Renee in particular for leaving me with her kids to raise. I wished God would give me about five minutes with them both, so I could give them each a good spanking, although I knew that all I would really do was hug and kiss them and tell them how glad I was to be back together again. I also felt angry toward Ken.

Because Ken and I expressed and dealt with our grief differently, I felt as if my husband didn't understand what I was going through, and he felt the same way about me. This experience heaped feelings of abandonment and loneliness on top of the pain we already felt. It was through our mutual anger, however, that I learned that people suffer and grieve in different ways.

There is no right or wrong way to grieve the loss of your loved ones. Still, for some reason, we tend to expect others to feel and act the same ways we do—and when they don't, we become frustrated and act out in anger. Since that realization, I have had to learn to let Ken grieve in his own way.

In fact, just the other day, he said to me, "There is no light at the end of this tunnel."

"Oh, yes, there is," I told him. "You just have to keep looking for it." Then I smiled to myself, because I knew that, in his own time, and with God's help, Ken would see it too.

Guilt and Emptiness

Anger made things worse for me too because it came with guilt. But then a lot of things about grief brought guilt with it. I felt guilty that, as a mother, I was not able to stop this horrible accident from happening. I told myself I should have known and been able to warn my daughters. I felt guilty that it was so hard to release my children and my pain to the Father. Then two years later, in 2005, when my mother passed away, I felt guilty because I could not handle going to her funeral.

I felt as though I had died on the side of the road that night, right along with my girls, and that my soul was buried with them in the grave. My body was here, but I was a shell, with nothing left but consuming emptiness.

Fortunately, coming to terms with this gaping hole inside me is what helped me reach out to God, and that is when I thought I could make out just the smallest pinprick of light at the end of my long, dark tunnel.

The following prayer is similar to what I offered up to God many, many times during this time in my life. You may be able to use parts of it in your own cries to the Father.

Oh, God, my children are gone, and I am weary and numb. I cannot imagine a grief worse than this. My heart is weeping, Lord, and only you can touch it and make it whole.

A deep hole was left in me when my beautiful daughters died on that horrible night, and that hole has not been filled. I need it to be filled with your Holy Spirit.

Lord, you have sent *Immanuel*, God with me. You have sent your Holy Spirit to comfort me. And I call upon the Comforter right now to visit the place where I am suffering, and I thank you, God, that just one touch of the Holy Spirit can change everything. There is no sweeter comfort than your presence. Lord, my greatest peace comes from you, and without you, I have no peace.

Lord, I am weary of the loads I am carrying. The business of living has drained the life out of me, and I am so tired. I don't need just sleep; I need real *rest*. My body, my mind, and my spirit need rest, and the only rest is in you, Lord.

Oh, Lord, bring your river of life to me and let it flow over me and refresh me so I can go on another day. Let it refresh every part of the weary, worn places in me.

Please send your Holy Spirit to comfort me and help me in a way I've never experienced. I need to know that you understand—really understand—what I am going through.

Being able to offer this prayer up was the beginning of my healing, but not the end of my pain. Remember, healing is a process; it takes time. Even today, I struggle with grief. In fact, I don't think that the pain is ever completely gone, but once you find hope, what pain is still there becomes manageable by trusting in God to get you through it.

Not long ago, a minister friend lost his son in a car accident. Many of our mutual friends tried to get me to call and talk with him and his wife, since I knew what it was like to be in their shoes. I didn't call. I knew they would not be able to hear me—not yet—because it always gets much worse before it starts to improve even a little.

A few months later, I saw them at a funeral, and she asked me, "When does it start to get better?"

"When I get there," I said, "I will let you know."

Finally, just as important as allowing yourself to grieve is letting yourself live again when it's time to come out of that tunnel. I struggled at that point in the road, afraid that if I really enjoyed anything in life that I was doing an injustice to my girls. After all, they were not there to enjoy life, so why should I be? But the truth was that I was doing them an injustice by not living, especially when it came to helping their children go on to enjoy life. I didn't realize, for example, how much I was actually hurting my granddaughters by being in such a state of depression.

I will always miss my beautiful daughters and granddaughter, and I will never stop loving them and remembering the wonderful life we shared together. But I must do all I can now to give their children some happy memories of their own. I must get beyond that accident and give my grandchildren the life their mothers would have wanted for them—and allow myself the life they would want for me.

Turn Tragedy Around

And we know that all things work together for good to them that love God,
to them who are the called according to his purpose.
–Romans 8:28

*G*etting through that tunnel of grief was, hands down, the hardest thing I have ever had to do. But as the saying goes, that which does not kill us makes us stronger. In other words, it is often the most challenging hardships in life that teach us the greatest lessons. So it's little wonder that I learned, and am still learning, a whole boat-load of lessons from this harrowing time in my life.

Although everyone's grief experience is different, I would like to use this chapter to pass along the major lessons I learned from my experience in hopes that at least some of them may also apply to your situation. Yes, sometimes there is no other way to *really* learn a lesson than the hard way. We have to walk through that refining fire ourselves to come out sharper. But if we can gain at least a little wisdom from someone else's mistakes or situation, it might help us navigate through the fire quicker. My prayer is that, by reading through the lessons I learned the hard way, you might gain insight into your unique grief experience and thus make your own trip through the tunnel shorter.

Lesson 1: Quit Pretending

I said this before, but I believe Christians have an easier time overcoming grief than those who do not believe because we know we don't have to go it alone. Even though we go through those times when we feel God isn't around, our faith often carries us through until it becomes clear that he is not only with us but always was. Christians who are assured that their loved ones were saved before they died can have even greater peace; they know that those loved ones are now in a place of no more pain and that they will see them again for eternity.

On the other hand, I think a lot of Christians have a harder time coping with the loss of loved ones because we somehow think that feeling extreme sadness or hopelessness or pain is sign of spiritual weakness. In my case, as a minister, I think I felt a double-dose of pressure to act strong, even when I didn't feel that way. I felt that I had to be strong for others, because it was my job to comfort everyone else. I also felt that I had to set a good example, literally practicing what I preached. I had always said to people, both in sermons and privately, "God will get you through anything." How could I show them that I was now struggling to believe that?

As Christians, we tend to think that, if we were trusting God the way we should be to get us through the situation, we wouldn't be feeling such intense grief. We wouldn't be questioning whether he was there with us at all times. So we try to act strong when really we are falling apart inside.

But what I learned through my experience is that it is actually pride—not trust in God—that keeps us pretending. Pride is what keeps us from letting on about how much we're struggling, and it's what prevents us from asking for, and then getting, the help we need. If we pretend that we are strong when, in fact, we are not, then we will not fully lean on God and his church the way God intended.

As such, pretending keeps us from fully healing the way we need to in order to be effective for his kingdom. We must use our pain, then, to learn to lean on God and on those who belong to him.

I can see now that it was not fair, either to me or to those in my congregation, for me to portray a false picture of myself. What people really needed to see was that it was okay to have feelings and to be vulnerable, and then to seek out the help that was needed. So it was no wonder I would end up feeling guilty whenever someone said, "I wish I could be as strong as you." Each such compliment was only a painful reminder that I was living a lie. I wanted to scream, "I am not strong. It is all an act. Actually, I am dying. Please, help me!" But my pride would not let me.

My redemption came in the fact that God didn't buy my act. He knew better. In fact, I later found out that he had people all over the United States praying for me—some I had never met. I got several phone calls from people saying, "Sister Thelma, you don't know me, but we know about you and your ministry, and we are praying for you." And then they backed up their prayers with actions.

So even if you're struggling with asking for help, don't ever think that God does not know the real you. Of course he does. And he will see you through.

Lesson 2: Don't Be a Slave to Circumstances

No one goes through life without at least a fair amount of stress, pain, heartache, and other negative experiences that come with living in this world. But these things do not have to control us or hinder our overall sense of peace and joy in life. We can still have joy on stressful days and peace in the middle of chaos. Why? Because *true* peace and joy are not given or taken by the world around us; rather, they come from God and lay within us. So unless we just hand the controls over to the world, our circumstances do not have to determine our inner sense of joy and peace.

In my experience, this God-given inner sense of peace amid turmoil was one of the first signs that I was emerging from the tunnel. My circumstances had not changed, but the way I began seeing them had. It reminded me of the story in Matthew 14:26–33:

And when the disciples saw him walking on the sea, they were troubled, saying, It is a spirit; and they cried out for fear. But straightway Jesus spake unto them, saying, Be of good cheer; it is I; be not afraid. And Peter answered him and said, Lord, if it be thou, bid me come unto thee on the water. And he said, Come. And when Peter was come down out of the ship, he walked on the water, to go to Jesus. But when he saw the wind boisterous, he was afraid; and beginning to sink, he cried, saying, Lord, save me. And immediately Jesus stretched forth his hand, and caught him, and said unto him, O thou of little faith, wherefore didst thou doubt? And when they were come into the ship, the wind ceased. Then they that were in the ship came and worshipped him, saying, Of a truth thou art the Son of God.

It was as if God had just showed up in that stormy sea of circumstances I was in and was calling me to walk across the tumultuous waters to come to him. Somehow, suddenly, I knew he would not let me drown.

That's not to say, however, that I never had my doubts. Like Peter, there were times when I found myself starting to sink. But it was through those times that I learned how to refocus on Jesus and then reach out for help. Each time, I found that Jesus was always right there, holding out his hand; it was just up to me to reach out and take it.

In other words, to maintain that continual sense of inner peace and joy, we must work at it. We must continually focus on Jesus, trust him to get us across whatever we may be facing at the moment, and then, when necessary, *choose* to reach out to him for help.

It's not always so easy, however. In fact, often, seeing and trusting God during difficult times is a process that we just have to work through. At times, we may find ourselves neck-deep in the water and gasping for air. We want to believe that Jesus will bring us through, but something in our lives is keeping us from doing so. At those times, we just have to go on with life and live it to best of our ability, knowing in our heads—even if we can't believe it in our hearts—that all things do work together for the good of those who love the Lord and are the called according to his purpose (Rom. 8:28). We might also take the advice of Philippians 4:8 and try to think positively. We can look for the good in every circumstance, even if it seems impossible to find—and believe me, there are times when it seems impossible to see any good. But the bottom line is that when we are struggling to believe God in our hearts, we must still hold onto God's Word in our minds and trust it to be true and faithful. Regardless of circumstances, we have to keep trying, and we have to keep choosing to follow God, and eventually we will see him on the waters ahead of us, calling us to him.

I remember times when my household seemed like a living hell. I had no spiritual help there, and there was constant cursing and griping and fighting. And yet I had peace in my heart through many of those days, because I had learned to make living for God not a condition of my circumstances, but a condition of my heart. I learned that I had to work at continually focusing on Christ.

As a pastor, I have heard so many people say, "If only my circumstances were different, I could live for God." "If only my husband understood me better," some might say, or "if only my children didn't require so much of my time and energy." But if you are looking for the perfect circumstances to live for God, then—I'm sorry for sounding blunt—but get ready to go to hell, because none of us will ever have the perfect circumstances in life.

Put another way, when we allow our circumstances to control how we think, act, or feel, we will end up like the children of Israel who died in the desert without ever reaching the Promised Land. Here,

God has freed us from slavery and is telling us that we can go to the Promised Land, but because we're so focused on the challenges that lay between here and there—that giant body of water up ahead and all those men on our tail—and not trusting God to get us through them, we forfeit the opportunity and the blessing. The children of Israel had everything they needed to make it to the Promised Land, but because they could not see the solutions to their problems right now, they gave up and started chasing idols. As he did for the Israelites, God will open up the waters for us, deal with anyone who is against us, and bring us to the Promised Land. We need only to trust him and keep diligently following his path.

Of course, the goal of the Promise Land means something different to each of us, but for me, it is ultimately heaven. That is where my dad, my mom, my children, and a couple of my grandkids are, not to mention all of my grandparents and two brothers-in-law. And I know that if I focus on Jesus and not on my circumstances, by the grace of God, I can make it there too.

Lesson 3: Choose Change

So many times, I would pray for my life to change and get better, but then I would run into the same troubles over and over again. For too long, I thought this was because God didn't want things to change—until it dawned on me that for God to answer my prayers, he had to be able to work in and through me—and he couldn't do that until I changed my ways. Here I had been praying for God to change my life, but I was not cooperating. I was doing and thinking and feeling the same things over and over and over again, and yet, for some odd reason, I was expecting different results. I was standing in my own way, and God was waiting for me to move.

I was being like the children of Israel who died in the wilderness because they never got their thinking out of Egypt. As slaves in Egypt, they had been told when to get up, when to work, when to eat, when to go home, and when to sleep. There was no thinking on their part; they just did what they were told. But in the wilderness, though they were free, they were not used to having to make their own decisions and be responsible for themselves.

As a result, they became a group a whining babies, blaming everyone else when the going got tough. It was all Moses's fault or God's fault, they'd say whenever they weren't making progress. And isn't that the way it is today? "I'm on drugs because my mom didn't love me," we often hear, or "I drink because my wife left me." Another common scapegoat: "I beat my kids because I was beat as a child." Though these may be legitimate reasons for why the behavior started, they most certainly are not legitimate excuses for not making those behaviors end. Change is always possible.

In order to see God's promise and to be fully delivered, the Israelites needed to change their thinking, their wills, and their emotions. Unfortunately for them, they refused. And it is the same for us today. If we, as Christians, do not change our wills and our ways of thinking—if we do not give up our slave mentality—then, like the Israelites, we will never be able to get to the Promised Land.

In my case, I was living a life of feeling defeated because of guilt and condemnation, which often came out in the form of sickness, anxiety attacks, and broken relationships. I was not living the life God had intended for me. But when I came out of that long, dark tunnel and began to see things for what they really were, I realized that I had to change to fulfill God's plan for my life. I knew God had not brought me out into the light just to watch me do things the same way I had always done them. I knew that if I wanted to honor God, and my children and grandchildren, I had to change and get control of my thoughts, will, and emotions.

In the process of trying to make this change happen, I have realized that there is no realm that Satan does not seek to control, most importantly our minds. That is why Romans 12:2 says, "And be not conformed to this world: but be ye transformed by the renewing of your mind, that ye may prove what is that good, and acceptable, and perfect, will of God." It is not God's will that his children be confused, tormented, or troubled with evil or negative thoughts. He wants us to have victory over our thought life as well as our emotions and our will.

That all sounds great, but is it possible? There were times in that tunnel when I didn't think so, and even today, I have fleeting moments of doubt. After all, we're talking about an incident so devastating and unthinkable that it can blow your mind. And if your mind is blown, how can you control your thoughts? But victory is possible. It is not easy, but it is possible—and the effort you put forth to get it is worth the reward.

Staying on top of our thought life is a daily process. The only place of operation the devil has is in our minds, and we have to give him permission to play on that playground. We must keep guard over our thoughts and continue to kick him out every time he tries to get in—as many times as that may be.

As a grieving person myself, I know you are probably saying, "I'm tired already!" But take heart: the process is easier once you learn how to get rid of Satan the instant you see him up to his old tricks. It's kind of like fleas on a dog. If you noticed your dog scratching, you might want to treat her for fleas as soon as possible. Otherwise, you might find yourself dealing not only with one flea, or even just a handful of them, but also with flea eggs, which hatch into more fleas, which produce even more eggs. And after all is said and done, you end up having to treat not only your dog but your entire house for months.

The same tip applies to dealing with your mind: when you detect what may seem like even the tiniest negative thought taking hold, you must get rid of it immediately. Otherwise you can be sure that it will breed more of the same, after which it will spread like wildfire—and at that point, you've got your work cut out for you.

It's time to get a grip and stop letting the devil get control of our thought life. And if he already has it, then it's time to get out the weapons of warfare and begin to take back what the devil has stolen. The weapons of our warfare, of course, are prayer and God's Word, and they are mighty at pulling down the strongholds of our mind, will, and emotions. Once those strongholds are down, we can take control of them again and surrender them to God—and I can tell you firsthand that God can and will do incredible things through us if we allow him access into our minds.

But I can also tell you firsthand that mind maintenance is not a perfect science, especially since we, as humans, are imperfect. Often it seems that we hardly think twice when Satan slips in a negative thought, but as soon as God tries to lead us in the direction of the Promised Land, we back off and cry for Egypt. But again, we must make a choice: either die in the desert or stop complaining and make it to the Promised Land.

When I feel overwhelmed with negative thoughts, I just remember that God knows I am human and can go off the deep end and that what matters is to get back on track and get my thinking under control. Because if Satan can make me think God has asked too much of me, and if he can make me believe I am unable to do what God has asked, then he can control my actions through my thoughts and turn me away from the very presence of God.

Maybe the hardest thing about change, in general, whether in our thoughts, emotions, or actions, is that it requires us to get out of our safety zone. When the water is raging all around and the waves knocking us from side to side, we just want to stay in the boat of comfort. But what God has shown me is that if we always stay in the boat, we will never be able to achieve the miracle of walking on water, which is just what Jesus is calling us to do. For it is exactly in those moments when we can't feel anything solid under our feet that we have to keep our eyes on Jesus and trust in him. And once the storm is over and we see that he didn't let us drown, our faith gets stronger, better preparing us for the next time around.

For those of us who are grieving, our comfort zone is that dark tunnel; though often overwhelming and depressing, it is also familiar. It's what we know and have grown accustomed to. So many times, I've wanted to crawl back into that dark, safe place. Sometimes it looks as if I'd be better off. But then I realize that's just another deceitful lie of the devil to make me think God is not capable of pulling me through.

In addition, now that I've reached the end of the tunnel, turning back would be a conscious decision. Before, when I was in the dark, I hadn't even realized that I had a choice to get out. I was still numb and blind. But in the light of day, my eyes were opened, and I realized that no one else on earth but me could get me out of this place in which I was stuck. I had to stop blaming my past and my circumstances for my actions and take the bull by the horns. Now I can readily acknowledge the fact that going back would be a deliberate choice to do something that's detrimental to myself, to my grandchildren, and to my congregation—because now, I know better. And when you know better, you do better.

So I continue to march forward, living by the serenity prayer, which says, "God, grant me the serenity to accept the things I cannot change, the courage to change the things I can, and the wisdom to know the difference." Because I not only need the courage to get out of my boat and change what I can; I also need the ability to decipher changes I can make from those I can't. There are, after all, some things in life we cannot control, and if we keep trying, it will only drive us crazy.

The bottom line: you can't do what you have always done and expect a different outcome. There comes a time when you have to get off the merry-go-round and do things differently. You have to stop blaming your mom or dad, your husband or wife, and definitely God for the way you are acting. You have realize that as long as you have someone or something to blame for the condition of your life, you will feel justified in living and feeling and thinking the way you do, and you will not change; after all, it's not your fault—someone or something else made you this way. And you have to come to terms with the fact that, if you want things to get better, you have to be the one to make the change.

Finally, once you have done all you can possibly do to stay standing, just rest on the Bible, which says it is now your time to stand and see the glory of God.

Lesson 4: Let Go

I am still learning this lesson. I know my three girls are with God, and I know I won't ever put my arms around them again in this life. But in my heart, I still struggle with turning them over to the care of God. I still find myself holding onto them, thinking that by some miracle, God will change his mind and send them back to me. In reality, I know that will never happen, but it's as if my mind can't help but play host to the fantasy.

It's like the commonly told parable about the jeweler: You take a broken watch to a jeweler. He tells you that he can fix it if you leave it with him, but then you turn around and take the watch home with you. Your watch is still broken. Who are you going to blame—yourself or the jeweler? In this instance, the answer is obvious. Yet in real life, we do the same thing with God. He tells us that if we lay our grief at his feet, he will fix it. But because of pride or self-will or some other reason, we pick it up and carry it around with us instead. Worse, we then often blame God when it's still a problem rather than taking the responsibility upon ourselves. But God cannot fix what we won't give him.

But Romans 10:10 tells us that there is a strong tie between what is believed and what is confessed: "[W]ith the heart man believeth unto righteousness; and with the mouth confession is made unto salvation." So I continue to confess this issue to the Lord and hope that, one day, I will be able to truly believe that I can let go of my girls.

Lesson 5: Remember God's Plan

When I was in that dark place, I often got caught up in feeling guilty for what had happened to my daughters and granddaughter. If I'd have only been a better person, I thought, they would still be alive. If I'd have had more faith, I could have kept them here, or if I'd been a better mom, Christian, human, and so on and so on. Looking back on that guilt, I now see it as almost a twisted form of selfishness. It was a signal that I somehow thought I was powerful enough to have caused this whole situation when in reality, I was not in control in any way.

As always, however, God *was* in charge. And so, naturally, I questioned why he allowed this tragedy to happen. My first and main question was why both of my daughters had to die at the same time. Second, I never understood why God would allow so much burden and responsibility to fall on my shoulders in the aftermath. I'd have never, in my worst nightmares, have imagined that I could stand losing one child, much less both at the same time. And never in a million years could I have guessed that I would face the kinds of challenges that I am dealing with now, much less get through them successfully. Raising teenagers in my sixties? No way.

But then, one day, I was looking through some old photos and noticed something that I had not paid attention to before. Almost every picture I had of Ragina and Renee were of them together. It dawned on me then that, just as my daughters were never separated in life, neither were they separated in death.

Maybe God knew that one of them could not have made it without the other, I thought, so *he let them go together.*

Maybe that wasn't the reason. Maybe God had another entirely different reason. But the important thing was that I finally realized that God had a bigger picture in mind, which I just couldn't see.

We tend to be so self-absorbed that we think we are the ones orchestrating everything in our lives. But what we need to remember is that man was never meant to stand alone. Adam and Eve were first created as companions to God. Unfortunately, they chose to listen to the counsel of Satan instead of the advice of their creator and thus ate from the tree of knowledge rather than the tree of life. Why? In short, Adam got a God-complex. He believed the serpent's lie that eating from the tree of knowledge would make him like God—and if he was like God, he could achieve independence from God and thus assert control over his own life.

Today, we are still buying the lie that we can be smart enough to be the god of our own lives. But whenever we try to live on our own, we fail miserably. We fail not only at whatever it is we are attempting but also bring misery upon ourselves and those around us. Just as it did for Adam and Eve, getting a God-complex is the surest way to destroy life as we know it, because there is only one God, and it's not you or me.

Even when we heed God's call for stable, constant faith, we often try to produce it ourselves. Faith is not something that is worked up; it isn't figuring out what you want and then believing it will happen. Faith is also not an emotional experience that gives us goose bumps, followed by our sincere attempts to make that feeling last. Quite simply, faith is God's gift of belief—belief that God will do what he said he would do in his Word. It is belief that he has a larger plan for our lives that we may not understand or agree with but that, nonetheless, exists for our benefit. And it is belief that, if we let him, he can turn even our worst circumstances and faults into something good.

Joseph was rejected by his brothers, thrown into a pit, sold into slavery, and put into prison because of a lie, but God used all of it together to fulfill the plan he had for Joseph's life—for Joseph to end up in a place of honor. Similarly, if we are willing to keep on fighting the good fight of faith and to relinquish control of our life to God, the pitfalls and disappointments we face will not stop him from fulfilling his plan for us. We can still have the Promised Land, no matter what comes our way.

In my case, I now know that God has planned a wonderful work to be done for his glory. So even while my mind is telling me that I won't be able to make it through, my spirit is leaping for joy, and I have the peace of knowing that God's will is God's bill—and he always pays. What, then, do I have to fear?

What the future holds, I do not know, but I do know that God will show me what path to take one day at a time, and that is the only way I can live anyway. What a wonderful feeling to know that God trusts me with the huge responsibility of being a vessel through which he can carry out his divine plan. Nothing I have ever done has felt that good.

Pay it Forward

And thou shalt be a blessing.
—Genesis 12:2

By the spring of 2009, my family life was well on its way toward recovery. The rat race was over, and we just had to learn to heal from the pain and anger, to move on, and to be as whole as possible as a family, even without Ragina, Renee, and Jessica. Of course, there would always be a hole in our lives because they were gone, but at least we had all found the hope of knowing that there was coming a reunion day, in which a sign would go up in each of our hearts, saying, ***"No vacancies for eternity."***

As for me, I had determined that I would try to use my experience to pass hope and help onto others. I had resolved to write this book and to create basic messages, based on the lessons I learned, that I could deliver in speeches and sermons. What I had not expected, however, was that I could also use the wisdom I'd gained in situations closer to home.

For example, one night recently, Sierra and I were crying together on the phone. She is ten now, and at the time, she was going through a period of missing her mom, so she wanted Grandma. But Grandma could not get to her right then because we live about twenty hours away from each other.

I'd been prepared for the conversation. Sierra's stepmom, Jeri, had told me ahead of time that Sierra had been missing her mom so much lately that she had wanted to back out of her project at the local fair. Sierra had been planning to show the baby lamb she had been raising, and up until this point, she had been very excited about the whole thing. Now Jeri was concerned.

So after Sierra and I cried together, I told her that it was okay to miss her mom and to be sad but that it was also important to count our blessings. And then I began to list them off for her, one by one. I said:

1. This time last year you were not in my life, and Grandma didn't even know where you were. But God let us find you, and he brought you home.
2. Now you have all of your mom's family back in your life, and no one can ever take you away from us and put you away again.
3. You are with your real dad and have a wonderful stepmom now, and they love you very much.
4. You have two brothers and a sister you didn't even know before, and now they are in your life and will love you and be with you forever.
5. Your real mom is looking down on you from heaven and will be so proud of you when you show your lamb at the fair this year. I just know she will be bragging all over heaven about her daughter taking her lamb to the fair.

"You're right, Grandma," Sierra said. "Grandma, will you pray for me?"

I smiled to myself. "Yes, I will, baby girl."

We prayed together on the phone, and when we finished, I talked to Jeri again, and I could tell that she had been there, crying right along with Sierra. Then, at some point during our conversation, Sierra chimed in in the background, and said, "Tell Grandma she made my day."

What a blessing to hear! In response, I told Jeri to relay the message that talking to Sierra had made my day too.

After we hung up, I couldn't help but wonder how different that conversation might have gone a year ago, when I had still been in the tunnel. Or how it would have been less positive had I allowed myself to get lost in a bottle of pills or given into the temptation to wander back into that dark place. In any one of those scenarios, I would not have been there for my granddaughter when she had needed me. Instead, I made a positive impact on her life. I was able to motivate her to change her mind, and to show up and participate—not just at the fair, but also, I hoped, in life.

Situations like these, I knew, were the reasons that I had to continue to fight to stay on this side of the tunnel. These were the reasons I had to continue to take my grief and pain and thoughts and baggage to Jesus daily. These were my reasons to keep moving on.

I know that God is working to transform my life continually and to keep my hope and faith alive. He stands ready to help me at all times if I only put my faith in him and trust him. God has entrusted me with a great work, and now I must trust him to perform it through me. Hope is the cord that connects us to heaven, and God takes the hopeless situations in our life and gives us hope in spite of them.

"Now unto him that is able to do exceeding abundantly above all that we ask or thank according to the power that worketh in us" (Eph. 3:20). *I was reading this, and all of a sudden it hit me that it's not through my power that I can do anything; it is the power of God working through me. If I am depending on his power, then I can have hope that everything will be all right.* It is when I start to feel as if I am responsible that I begin to feel hopeless, because within me there is no strength, but it is God's strength that works in me. If that doesn't free you up from a lot of baggage, nothing will. It's not by might or by power but by my spirit, says the Lord. These mountains will be removed.

If you have lost a child, you will never be the same, but allow the grief and the pain because that is what will heal you. Go ahead and throw rocks; I have even thrown dishes. It's okay. (Just not at someone, okay?) But you get it. God knows your grief. I thought for years I was being unfaithful to God when I was not able to function in the normal world. Then I asked myself, "What's normal?" If you can answer that question, please give me the answer. Walk in love, and everything else will come. A man in my church in Spiro once said, "To live above with saints we love, now this is grand and glory, but to live below with saints we know—well that's another story." How true that is. But I believe it's because we are always trying to change people to suit us and not allowing God to change them to suit him.

If you take one thing from all we have faced, I pray it is the realization that God can and will see you through every trial of your life. That joy is not a laugh or smile; it's in knowing that God took the crown of thorns so we could partake of the joy of knowing no matter what our circumstances are, God is right there with us.

In Habakkuk 3:17–18, the prophet said, "Although the fig tree shall not blossom, neither shall fruit be in the vines; the labor of the olive shall fail and the fields shall yield no meat; the flock shall be cut off from the fold and there shall be no herd in the stalls yet will I rejoice in the Lord. I will joy in God, the God of my salvation."

Be assured of one thing: we can triumph in our troubles. Romans 5:3–4 means to me that pressure, affliction, and hardships produce patience and endurance. They develop character that is approved faith, and character of this type produces the habit of joyful and confident hope in God. The schemes of the enemy serve only to develop us for our destiny.

Update

On May 24, 2011, an F5 tornado hit our home. It took everything, even the trees, cars, and fence posts. We have not rebuilt yet. We are still waiting on that miracle, but we know it is coming. I'm reminded of a song I heard years ago that says, "There's a miracle in the making." We are all doing well and asking God to take our lives in the ups and downs, the good, the bad, and the ugly. I hope it will somehow show you, the reader, that you have a miracle on its way. Don't be afraid to trust, even if your eyes are seeing an impossible situation, because God takes the impossible and makes it possible.

I look at all the pictures, or at least the ones that didn't get blown away by the F5 tornado. We are looking for a house now, but finding the quality of home we had is going to be very hard. We have looked, but for what God has in mind for that place, I just can't find the right place or at the right price. I am trying to be the voice of reason and let my family know God has a plan and we hold the key. I went running the other morning, but I was pacing by myself and feeling clean. But I try to analyze every word and not just let it fall out.